John S. Inskip

Songs of Triumph

adapted to prayer meetings, camp meetings, and all other seasons of

religious worship

John S. Inskip

Songs of Triumph
adapted to prayer meetings, camp meetings, and all other seasons of religious worship

ISBN/EAN: 9783337265786

Printed in Europe, USA, Canada, Australia, Japan

Cover: Foto ©Lupo / pixelio.de

More available books at **www.hansebooks.com**

SONGS OF TRIUMPH:

ADAPTED TO

PRAYER MEETINGS, CAMP MEETINGS, AND ALL OTHER
SEASONS OF RELIGIOUS WORSHIP.

SELECTED & ARRANGED

–BY–

REV. J. S. INSKIP.

———•———

921 ARCH ST., PHILADELPHIA:
National Publishing Association for the Promotion of Holiness.

PREFACE.

———o———

"O clap your hands, all ye people; shout unto God with the voice of triumph."—Ps. 47: 1.

"Now thanks be unto God, which always causeth us to triumph in Christ."—2 Cor. 2: 14.

Ages ago the prophet predicted that the "ransomed of the Lord," walking in the Highway of Holiness, "shall return, and come to Zion with songs and everlasting joy upon their heads." Those who are journeying in this way, we trust will find much help and comfort in singing "SONGS OF TRIUMPH." The great variety of *favorites* from various sources, and the unusual amount of entirely new pieces, it is believed will make the collection one of the most popular and effective that has been published. God grant that all who sing these "SONGS OF TRIUMPH," may take part in the "Song of Moses and the Lamb."

Philadelphia, May 1, 1882.

J. S. INSKIP.

SONGS OF TRIUMPH.

No. 1.

FANNY J. CROSBY.

LIFT THE CROSS.

W. J. KIRKPATRICK. By per.

1. O ye watchman sound the trum-pet, Sound it far . . and
2. See Him rid-ing on to con-quor; See a count-less
3. See their ar-mor, how it glit-ters In the morn-ing
4. Ev-'ry foe shall yet be van-quished Strife and wrong shall

near, Lo! the morn of gos-pel free-dom Comes the world to cheer.
throng; Swell their ranks and while they fol-low, Hear the migh-ty song.
light, While the pow'rs of sin and darkness Tremble at the sight.
cease, All the world shall own His cep-tre, Christ the Prince of Peace.

REFRAIN.

Lift the cross and wave its ban-ner; Shout the joy-ful

strain, Christ the Lord, the King of Glo-ry, O-ver all shall reign.

No. 2. SALVATION FREE AND FULL.

Written for, and sung during "The Evangelistic Tour round the World."

MARY D. JAMES.　　　　　　　　　　　　　　W. J. KIRKPATRICK. By per.

1. Lo, we come to preach glad tidings, Je - sus' untold love to show!
2. Wondrous love! a-maz-ing mer - cy! Sin - ners, Je-sus can transform;
3. We would tell of countless treas-ures In His boundless stores of grace!
4. Fa - ther, Son, and Holy Spir - it, All combined to save the lost;
5. Come, then, to our glorious Sav - iour! Now He's waiting to re-ceive

His unmeasured wealth of mer - cy, We would have the world to know.
Thro' the precious blood and spir - it To a saint ex - alt a worm.
All for you, those stores so precious, If His of - fers you em - brace.
All may have this great sal - va - tion, Purchased at such priceless cost!
Ev - 'ry soul that seeks His fa - vor, All who in His name be - lieve.

REFRAIN.

Free sal- va - tion! Full sal-va - tion! Glorious tidings to the nations we pro-

claim; Par - don, pur - i - ty, and heav - en Thro' the

mer - its of the great Re-deemer's name. Hal - le - lu - jah, Hal - le -

4

SALVATION FREE AND FULL. Concluded.

lu - jah, Hal - le - lu - jah, Praise the dear a-ton- ing Lamb,

Praise the Lamb!

No. 3.   OH! 'TIS GLORY IN MY SOUL.

FLORA L. BEST.

JNO. R. SWENEY. By per.

1. To Thy cross, dear Christ, I'm clinging, All my refuge and my plea; Matchless
2. Long my heart hath heard Thee calling, But I thrust aside Thy grace; Yet, O
3. Love e- tern - al, light e-tern- al, Close me safe - ly, sweetly in; Sav-iour,

REFRAIN.

is Thy loving kindness, Else it had not stoop'd to me. Oh, 'tis glory! oh, 'tis glory! oh,
boundless condescension, Love is shining from Thy face.   ['tis
let Thy balm of healing, Ever keep me free from sin.

glory in my soul, For I've touched the hem of His garment, And his pow'r doth
[make me whole.

From "GEMS OF PRAISE."

5

No. 4. TRUSTING JESUS, THAT IS ALL.

EDGAR PAGE.   JNO. R. SWENEY. By per.

1. Sim - ply trusting ev - 'ry day;   Trusting, tho' a stormy way;
2. Brightly doth His Spir - it shine   In - to this poor heart of mine;
3. Sing - ing, if my way is clear;   Pray - ing, if the path is drear;
4. Trusting as the moments fly,   Trut - ing as the days go by,

E - ven when my faith is small,   Trust - ing Je - sus, that is all.
While he leads, I can - not fall,   Trust - ing Je - sus, that is all.
If   in danger, for Him call—   Trust - ing Je - sus, that is all.
Trusting Him, whate'er befall—   Trust - ing Je - sus, that is all.

REFRAIN.

Trusting him while life shall last,   Trusting him till earth is past—
    life shall last,   earth is past,

Till within the jasper wall—   Trusting Je - sus, that is all.
    jasper wall,

From "Gems of Praise."   Copyright, 1874, by JNO. R. SWENEY.

-6-

No. 5. HE IS MY PORTION FOREVER.

LIZZIE EDWARD.   JNO. R. SWENEY. By per.

1. All, all to Je - sus, I   consecrate anew, He is my portion for - ev - er;
2. All, all to Je - sus, my trusting heart can say, He is my portion forev - er;
3. Though He may try me this blessed truth I know, He is my portion forever;
4. All, all to Je - sus, I   cheerfully resign, He is my portion for - ev - er;

On - ly His glory, henchforth will I pursue, He is my portion forev - er.
Led by His mercy I'm walking ev'ry day, He is my portion forev - er.
He will not leave me, His promise tells me so, He is my portion forev - er.
I have the witness that He, my Lord, is mine, He is my portion forev - er.

REFRAIN.

Take, take the world with all its gilded toys, Take, take the world I covet not its joys.

Mine is a wealth no moth nor rust destroys; Jesus my portion forev - er.

7

No. 6.   # WORK FOR JESUS.

Rev. E. H. Stokes, D. D.   Wm. G. Fischer.   By per.

1. We have toil'd in ma-ny vineyards, We have toil'd thro' many a day,
2. We have toil'd thro' storm and sunshine, Summer's heat, and winter's cold;
3. We have toil'd in hu-man gardens, Dig-ging, sow-ing, pruning, too,
4. Lo! the gar-dens blooms with flowers, Fragance fills the blessed air;

Toil'd for thee, O bless-ed Je-sus, Worn for thee our strength away.
Toil is sweet in youth's bright morning, Sweet when men are growing old.
Pray-ing for the dew and sunshine, On the work we found to do.
Liv-ing, dy-ing, precious brethren, Toil for Je-sus ev-'ry where.

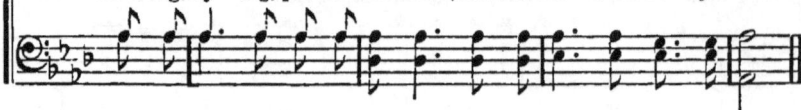

REFRAIN.

And we still will work for Je-sus, Work for Him has blessed pay;

We will ev-er work for Je-sus, Work for Him our lives a-way.

No. 7. GATHERING JEWELS.

Miss P. J. Owens.　　　　　　　　　　W. J. Kirkpatrick. By per.

1. Jew - el-gatherers for a crown, Know ye not that many a gem,
2. Souls for whom the Saviour died, Souls enwrapped in sin-ful night,
3. Gems by cru - el hands defaced, Pearls in heathen shadows dim,
4. With His blood washed bright and pure, Graven with His name divine,
5. Then our work shall be complete, Then we'll lay our off'rings down,

Now in darkness trampled down, Might bedeck a di - a - dem.
Go and seek them far and wide, They will glit-ter in His sight.
Brilliants scattered in the waste, We must gather up for Him.
These our jew-els shall en-dure, When the stars shall cease to shine.
We will lay them at His feet, He will lift them to His crown.

REFRAIN.

Gathering jewels, precious jewels, Blood bought souls we seek to bring.

Gathering jewels, precious jewels, For the crown of Christ our King.

9

No. 8. THE CHILD OF A KING.

HATTIE E. BUELL.   REV. JNO. B. SUMNER. By per.

1. My Fa - ther is rich in hous - es and lands, He
2. My Fa - ther's own Son, the Sa - viour of men! Once
3. I once was an out - cast, stran - ger on earth, A
4. A tent or a cot - tage, why should I care? They're

hold-eth the wealth of the world in his hands! Of ru-bies and diamonds, of
wander'd on earth as the poor-est of men, But now He is reign-ing for-
sin - ner by choice and an "al - ien" by birth, But I've been "adopt-ed," my
build-ing a pal-ace for me o'- ver there! Tho' ex - iled from home, yet,

sil - ver and gold: His cof-fers are full, He has rich-es un-told.
ev - er on High, And will give us a home in the sweet by and by.
name's writ-ten down: An heir to a mansion, a robe and a crown.
still I may sing: All glo - ry to God, I'm the child of a King.

REFRAIN.

I'm the child of a King, The child of a King,

With Je - sus my Sa - viour, I'm the child of a King.

10

No. 9. WHILE THE DAYS ARE GOING BY.

GEORGE COOPER. By per.   JNO. R. SWENEY. By per.

Recitante.

1. There are lonely hearts to cherish, While the days are going by; There are
2. There's no time for i - dle scorning, While the days are going by; Let our
3. All the loving links that bind us While the days are going by; One by

weary souls who perish While the days are going by. If a smile we can renew,
face be like the morning, While the days are going by. Oh, the world is full of sighs,
one we leave behind us While the days are going by. But the seeds of good we sow,

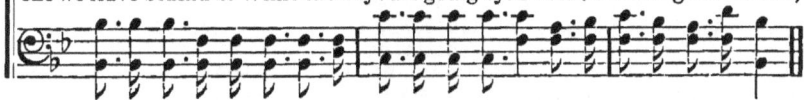

As our journey we pursue, Oh, the good that we may do, While the days are going by.
Full of sad and weeping eyes; Help your fallen brother rise While the days are go-
[ing by.
Both in shade and shine will grow, And will keep our hearts aglow, While the days
[are going by.

REFRAIN.

While go - ing   by,   While go - ing   by,
   While go - ing   by,   While go - ing   by,

Oh,   the   good we may   be   doing, While the days   are   going   by.

11

I BELIEVE.

R. KELSO CARTER. By per.

1. I believe that God in mer-cy, Has a wondrous work begun;
2. I believe that all are sinners; But the promise is so free—
3. I believe sal - va - tion's offered, Without mon - ey, without cost,
4. I believe, oh! Lord my Sa-viour, Help mine un - be - lief I pray,

And that souls, from sin's dark bondage, May by sovereign love be won;
"Who - so - ev - er will"—ah! surely, "Who - so - ev - er" includes me!
To the wea - ry, heav - y lad - en, Wand'ring, homeless, tempest-toss'd.
That I now have life e - ter - nal, Not to-mor-row, but to day.

I believe He sent a Saviour, Sent His own be - lov - ed Son.
I believe Christ died for sinners, I believe He died for me.
I believe that Je - sus on - ly Came to seek and save the lost.
I believe the words of Je - sus, I believe I'm saved to day.

REFRAIN.

I believe, yes, I believe, Help mine un - be - lief, O Lord!

Copyright, 1882, by JNO. R. SWENEY

12.

No. 11.   WHY NOT NOW?

Mrs. Mary D. James.   W. J. Kirkpatrick. By per.

Flowingly.

1. Why not now? The Spirit's pleading, Now the Saviour's in-ter-ceding,
2. Why not now take sweetest pleasures? Why not now grasp richest treasures?
3. Why not now? The time is fly-ing! Earthly things are fading, dy-ing!

Now He bids you come! Mercy, boundless mercy's flowing, Love in Je-sus'
Why not, while you may? Now Heav'n's purest joys are offered, Now its priceless
All will soon be o'er! Fleeting as the dews of morning, Death on ev'ry

heart is glowing, Come! oh, now come home! Come! oh, now come home!
gifts are proffered; Seize the prize today! Seize the prize to-day!
side is warning! Cling to earth no more. Cling to earth no more!

REFRAIN.

Why not now, why not now, Why not be saved just now?

Why not now, why not now, Why not be saved just now?

Just now?

CLEANSING WAVE.

Mrs. Phoebe Palmer.

Mrs. Jos. F. Knapp. By per.

1. Oh, now I see the crimson wave, The fountain deep and wide, Je-
2. I see the new cre - a-tion rise, I hear the speaking blood; It
3. I rise to walk in heaven's own light, Above the world and sin, With
4. A - mazing grace! 'tis heaven below, To feel the blood applied; And

sus, my Lord, might-y to save, Points to his wound-ed side.
speaks! pol-lut - ed na - ture dies! Sinks 'neath the cleansing flood.
heart made pure, and garments white, And Christ enthroned with-in.
Je - sus, on - ly Je - sus know, My Je - sus cru - ci - fied.

Refrain.

The cleansing stream, I see, I see! I plunge, and Oh, it cleanseth me! Oh,

praise the Lord, it cleanseth me! It cleanseth me, yes, cleanseth me!

14

No. 13.   ## ALL ARE MINE.

Rev. E. H. Stokes, D. D.   W. J. Kirkpatrick. By per.

1. All are mine, thou ho - ly Je-sus, All thy bless - ed words di-vine;
2. All thy prom - is - es of par-don, Com-ing from the throne a - bove,
3. All thy prom - is - es of com-fort. Ev - 'ry prom - ise of re - lief ;
4. All thy prom - is - es e - ter - nal, Hon-ored in the a - ges past,

All thy prom - is - es of fa-vor, All are mine, for - ev - er mine.
All thy prom - is - es of cleansing, All thy prom - is - es of love.
All thy prom - is - es of gladness, Prom-is - es of joy in grief.
Words which must remain un-brok-en, Prom-is - es of heav'n at last.

REFRAIN.

All are mine, Oh, matchless mercy ! Oh, how boundless is the store !

All thy prom - is - es of fa - vor, All are mine for ev - er more.

No. 14. WHAT A GATH'RING THAT WILL BE.

J. H. K.

J. H. KURZENKNABE. By per.

1. At the sounding of the trumpet, when the saints are gather'd home, We will
2. When the an-gel of the Lord proclaims that time shall be no more, We shall
3. At the great and final judgment, when the hidden come to light, When the
4. When the golden harps are sounding, and the angel bands proclaim, In tri-

greet each other by the crystal sea, With the friends and all the lov'd ones there a-
gather, and the saved and ransom'd see, Then to meet again together, on the
Lord in all His glory we shall see, At the bidding of our Saviour, "Come ye
umphant strains the glorious jubilee, Then to meet and join to sing the song of
crystal sea.

wait-ing us to come, What a gath'ring of the faithful that will be.
bright ce - les - tial shore, What a gath'ring of the faithful that will be.
bless - ed to my right," What a gath'ring of the faithful that will be.
Mo - ses and the Lamb, What a gath'ring of the faithful that will be.

REFRAIN.

What a gath - - - 'ring, gath - - - 'ring, At the
What a gath'ring of the loved ones when we'll meet with one an - oth - er,

sounding of the glorious ju-bi-lee! What a gath - - - 'ring,
ju - bi-lee! What a gath'ring when the friends and all the

From "Song Treasury"

WHAT A GATH'RING THAT WILL BE. Concluded.

gath   'ring, What a gath-'ring of the faith-ful that will be.
dear ones meet each oth-er

No. 15.   PRECIOUS STREAM.

H. L. G.   H. L. GILMOUR.   By per.

1. A stream from Calv'ry's summit rolls, Where all the weary, wand'ring souls,
2. That stream of liv-ing wa-ter flows Where oft' the weary pilgrim goes,
3. Flow on, thou stream; oh, ceaseless flow, 'Till ev'ry child of sin and woe
4. Oh! thoughtless soul, why longer wait? Why trifle on the brink of fate?

FINE.

And who-so-ev-er thirsts to-day, May drink and find Christ precious.
To drink, and quench his rag-ing thirst, And find his Sav-iour precious.
Hath plunged beneath thy cleansing tide, And found his Sav-iour precious.
That stream still flows for you and me, Oh, come and find Christ precious.

D.S. love to drink and sat-is-fy My thirst-ing soul with Je-sus.

REFRAIN.   D. S.

Oh! precious Je-sus, Rock for me, Stream in a des-ert boundless, free; I

No. 16. IT IS GOOD TO BE HERE.

Rev. Isaac N. Wilson.   Jno. R. Sweney. By per.

1. { While we bow in Thy name, O meet us a-gain, Fill our
   { May the Spir-it of grace, and the smiles of Thy face, Gent-ly
2. { Our souls long for Thee; O may we now see A sin-
   { And feel as it rolls in pow'r o'er our souls. It is
3. { Thou art with us, we know; we feel the sweet flow Of the
   { We are wash'd from our sin, made all ho-ly with-in, And in

D.S. light streaming down makes the pathway all clear, It is

Fine. Refrain.

hearts with the light of Thy love. }
fall on us now from a-bove. } It is good to be here, it is
cleansing blood wave ap - pear. }
good for us, Lord, to be here. }
sin cleansing wave's gladd'ning tide; }
Je - sus we sweetly a - bide. }

good for us, Lord, to be here.

D.S.

good to be here, Thy perfect love now drives a-way all our fear, And

No. 17.   *Tune and Chorus.—"It is Good to be Here."*

1. O how happy are they
   Who the Saviour obey,
   And have laid up their treasures above;
   Tongue can never express
   The sweet comfort and peace
   Of a soul in its earliest love.

2. That sweet comfort was mine,
   When the favor divine   [Lamb;
   I received through the blood of the
   When my heart first believed,
   What a joy I received—
   What a heaven in Jesus' name!

3. 'Twas a heaven below
   My Redeemer to know,
   And the angels could do nothing more
   Than to fall at His feet,
   And the story repeat,
   And the Lover of sinners adore.

4. Jesus, all the day long,
   Was my joy and my song;
   O, that all His salvation might see:
   He hath loved me, I cried,
   He hath suffered and died,
   To redeem even rebels like me.

18

TAKE ME AS I AM.

ANON. REV J. H. STOCKTON. Arr by W. J. K.

1. Je-sus, my Lord, to thee I cry, Un-less thou help me I must die;
2. Help-less I am, and full of guilt, But yet for me Thy blood was spilt,
3. I thirst, I long to know Thy love, Thy full salvation I would prove;
4. If Thou hast work for me to do, In-spire my will, my heart renew
5. And when at last the work is done, The bat-tle o'er the vic-t'ry won,

:S: FINE.

Oh, bring Thy free sal-va-tion nigh, And take me as I am!
And Thou can'st make me what Thou wilt, And take me as I am!
But since to Thee I can-not move, Oh, take me as I am!
And work both in and by me too, But take me as I am!
Still, still my cry shall be a-lone, O, take me as I am!

D.S. bring Thy free sal-va-tion nigh, And take me as I am!

REFRAIN. D. S.:S:

Take me as I am, Take me as I am; Oh,
Take me as I am, Take me as I am;

From "The Garner." By per. of JNO. J. HOOD.

No. 19. *Tune and Chorus—"Take Me as I Am."*

1. Just as I am, without one plea,
   But that Thy blood was shed for me,
   And that Thou bid'st me come to thee,
   O Lamb of God, I come!

2. Just as I am, and waiting not
   To rid my soul of one dark blot, [spot,
   To Thee, whose blood can cleanse each
   O Lamb of God, I come!

3. Just as I am, though tossed about
   With many a conflict, many a doubt,
   Fightings within, and fears without,
   O Lamb of God, I come!

4. Just as I am, poor, wretched, blind,
   Sight, riches, healing of the mind,
   Yea, all I need in Thee to find,
   O Lamb of God, I come!

5. Just as I am, thou wilt receive,
   Wilt welcome, pardon, cleanse, relieve,
   Because thy promise I believe,
   O Lamb of God, I come!

6. Just as I am, thy love unknown
   Hath broken every barrier down;
   Now, to be thine, and thine alone,
   O Lamb of God, I come!

THE NEW SONG.

Flora L. Best.

Jno. R. Sweney. By per.

Moderato.

1. There are songs of joy that I loved to sing, When my heart was blithe as a
2. There are strains of home that are dear as life, And I list to them oft 'mid the
3. Can my lips be mute, or my heart be sad, When the gracious Mas-ter hath
4. I shall catch the gleam of its jasper wall When I come to the gloom of the

bird   in Spring; But the song I have learned is so full of cheer, That the
din   of strife; But I know of a home that is wondrous fair, And I
made   me glad? When he points where the many mansions be, And
e - ven - fall, For I know that the shadows, dreary and dim, Have a

REFRAIN. *Vivace.*

dawn shines out in the darkness drear.
sing the psalm they are singing there. O, the new,   new song!   O, the
sweetly says, 'There is one for thee?'   O, the new,   new song!
path of light that will lead to Him.

new,   new song,   I can sing   it now   With the
O, the new,   new song,   I can sing   just now With the

From "Gems of Praise,"

THE NEW SONG. Concluded.

ran - - som'd throng: ... Power and dominion to him that shall
ransom'd, the ransom'd throng : ...

reign; Glo - ry and praise to the Lamb that was slain.
that shall reign;

No. 21. GIVE ME JESUS.

Fanny J. Crosby.

Jno. R. Sweney. By per.

FINE.

1. { Take the world, but give me Je - sus—All its joys are but a name; }
   { But his love a - bi - deth ev - er, Through e - ter - nal years the same. }
2. { Take the world, but give me Je - sus, Sweetest comfort of my soul; }
   { With my Saviour watching o'er me I can sing, though billows roll. }

D.C. O the fullness of redemption, Pledge of end - less life a - bove.

REFRAIN.

D.C.

O the height and depth of mercy, O the length and breadth of love.

3.
Take the world, but give me Jesus,
Let me view His constant smile;
Then throughout my pilgrim journey
Light will cheer me all the while.

4.
Take the world, but give me Jesus;
In His cross my trust shall be,
Till, with clearer, brighter vision,
Face to face my Lord I see.

No. 22. HEM OF HIS GARMENT.

W. J.

Wm. Johnson By per.

1. Weak and weary, poor and sinful, Vainly I cry; Bound and crush'd with
2. How the people press around Him, His word receive; Sure-ly I may
3. Long my heart has felt its burden, Seeking for peace; Now, at last I

years of sorrow, What help is nigh? Let me touch the hem of His
share His blessing I too believe.
find in Je-sus My sweet release.

REFRAIN.

Let me touch the hem of His

garment, Let me touch the hem of His garment, Let me

touch the hem of His garment, And the touch will make me whole.

JOY IS TEEMING.

Dr. Geo. P. Oliver.   W. J. Kirkpatrick. By per.

1. Tell me not my   lot   is sad - ness, Now I've gain'd this state so
2. Calm-ly are the   mo-ments fly - ing, Free from ev -'ry care and
3. Free from ev -'ry earth - ly bil - low, Now my wea-ry head may

bright; Ev'ry thought is filled with gladness, Life is now one scene of light.
fear; Precious Je-sus, when I'm dy - ing, Let me feel Thee then as near.
rest; Let me make my la - test pil - low, On my dear Redeemer's breast.

Refrain.

Joy is teeming, joy is teeming without measure, Sweetly in   my throbbing
without measure, sweetly teeming in my throbbing

heart; Seal, oh, seal the heav'nly treas - ure, Let   it nev-er from me part.
heart.

From "Leaflet Gems, No. 2."

No. 24. COMPANIONSHIP WITH JESUS.

MARY. D. JAMES. W. J. KIRKPATRICK. By per.

1. Oh, bles - sed fel - low-ship di - vine! Oh, joy supremely sweet! Com-
2. I'm walk - ing close to Je - sus' side, So close that I can hear The
3. I'm lean - ing on His lov - ing breast, A-long life's weary way; My
4. I know His shel-t'ring wings of love Are al-ways o'er me spread, And

pan - ion - ship with Je - sus here Makes life with bliss re-plete, In
soft - est whisp - ers of His love, In fel - low-ship so dear, And
path, il - lum - ined by His smiles, Grows brighter day by day, No
tho' the storms may fierce-ly rage, All calm and free from dread, My

un - ion with the pur - est one I find my heav'n on earth be-gun.
feel His great al-might - y hand Protects me in this hos - tile land.
foes, no woes my heart can fear, With my al-might - y Friend so near.
peace-ful spir - it ev - er sings "I'll trust the cov - ert of Thy wings.

REFRAIN.

Oh, wondrous bliss! oh, joy sublime! I've Je - sus with me all the time!

Oh, wondrous bliss! oh joy sub-lime I've Je - sus with me all the time.

24

No. 25.   # HAPPY TIDINGS.

Lizzie Edwards.   Jno. R. Sweney. By per.

1. Tidings, happy tidings, Hark! hark! the sound! Hear the joyful ech - o
2. Tidings, happy tidings, Hark! hark! they say, Do not slight the warning,
3. Tidings, happy tidings, Hark! hark! a-gain! Rushing o'er the mountain,

Through the world resound; Christ the Lord proclaims them, Hear and heed the call,
Come, O come to day. Christ, our loving Sav-iour, Still re-peats the call—
Sweeping o'er the plain; Onward goes the mes-sage, 'Tis the Saviour's call,

REFRAIN.

Come ye starving ones that perish, Room, room for all. Whoso-ev-er ask-eth,
Come ye wea-ry hea-vy la-den, Room, room for all.
Come for ev-'ry thing is ready, Room, room for all.

Je - sus will re-ceive; Who-so-ev-er thirst-eth Je - sus will re-lieve.

See the living waters Flowing full and free, O the blessed whosoever, That means me.

Copyright, 1882, by Jno. R. Sweney.
25.

No. 26. THE FAIR LAND OF SONG.

FANNY J. CROSBY.   JNO. R. SWENEY. BY per.

1. How bright is our prospect, O soldiers of Jesus, While homeward to zion we're
2. O be not discouraged, though arrows are flying, And fearful the contest twixt
3. Though truth on the field for a moment lies bleeding, See proudly she rises her
4. O sweet is the thought, and still brighter the prospect, The war will be over the

marching along, Each day brings us nearer the end of our journey, Each
right and the wrong, Stand fast by our colors, for on-ly the faith-ful Tri-
armies are strong, Her cause shall prevail and her val-ient de-fenders Re-
time is not long, 'Till glo-ry to Jesus and praise for the conquest, We'll

D.S. day brings us nearer the end of our journey, Each

FINE. REFRAIN.

day brings us nearer, the fair land of song.   The fair land of song, The
umphant shall enter, the fair land of song.
joic-ing shall enter, the fair land of song.
shout as we enter, the fair land of song.

day brings us nearer the fair land of song.

D.S.

dear land of song; To meet our Redeemer we're marching along; Each

No. 27.

MORE LIKE THEE.

W. J. K.

W. J. KIRKPATRICK. By per.

1. Je - sus, Sav-iour, great Ex-am - ple, Pattern of all pu - ri - ty,
2. Lest I wan - der from Thy pathway, Or my feet move wear-i - ly,
3. When tempta-tions fiercely low - er, And my shrinking soul would flee,
4. When around me all is darkness, And Thy beauties none may see,
5. When death's cold, repulsive fin - ger Leaves its impress on my brow,

I would fol - low in Thy footseps, Dai - ly growing more like Thee.
Saviour, take my hand and lead me, Keep me steadfast: more like Thee.
Change each weakness in - to pow - er, Keep me spotless: more like Thee.
May Thy beams, O Glorious Brightness, In effulgence shine through me.
May Thy life, with - in me swelling, Keep me singing then as now.

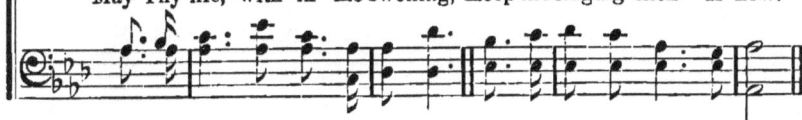

REFRAIN.

More like Thee, more like Thee, Saviour, this my constant pray'r shall be,
More like Thee. more like Thee,

Day by day, where'er I stay, Make me more, and more like Thee.

Copyright. 1876, by W. J. KIRKPATRICK.

27

No. 28.   SUFFICIENT FOR ME!

Miss P. J. Owens.　　　　　　　　　　　　W. J. Kirkpatrick. By per.

1. "My grace is suf-ficient for thee:" I sing the sweet words o'er and o'er;
2. Suf-ficient to cleanse, and to keep My hunger and thirst all supplied,
3. Each day has its tri-als and cares, Each day has its help for my need,
4. His might shall my weakness sustain, His fulness my portion shall be,

His promise my comfort shall be, The strength of my heart evermore.
The fountain of mercy is deep, The streams of salvation are wide.
Each pathway its thorns and its snares, But I sing while His promise I read.
His pow'r is made perfect in pain, His purpose made perfect in me.

REFRAIN.

Suf - fi - cient for me, suf - fi - cient for me, His

grace so a - bundant and free, In sor-row or pain this

Joy shall re-main, His grace is suf - fi - cient for me.
for me.

No. 29. THY PRECIOUS, PRECIOUS FOLD.

SALLIE SMITH.

JNO. R. SWENEY. By per.

1. Saviour, though long I have slighted Thee, Still Thou hast kind-ly in-
2. No more the night cometh drear-i - ly, No more my feet wan-der
3. Saviour, how gent - ly Thou guidest me, How in Thy mer - cy Thou
4. Saved by Thy grace, and so ten - der - ly, Glo-ry and praise I will

vited me, Praise for the love that united me To Thy precious, precious fold
wear-i-ly, Sweet is Thy voice and how cheeri-ly It has led me to Thy fold.
hidest me, All that I need Thou providest me, In Thy precious, precious fold.
render Thee, Thou in Thy mercy remembered me, Thou hast brought me to Thy
[fold.

REFRAIN.

I am hap - py now, I am hap - py now, How my

heart is swell - ing, all His mer - cy tell - ing; I am

hap - py now, I am hap-py now, In Thy precious, pre-cious fold.

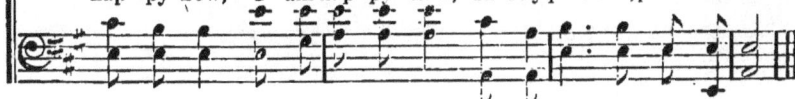

No. 30.   REDEEMED.

FANNY J. CROSBY.   W. J. KIRKPATRICK.   By per.

1. Redeemed, how I love to proclaim it, Redeemed by the blood of the Lamb; Re-
2. Redeemed, and so happy in Jesus, No language my rapture can tell, I
3. I think of my blessed Redeemer, I think of Him all the day long, I
4. I know I shall see in His beauty, The King in whose law I delight, Who
5. I know there's a crown that is waiting In yonder bright mansion for me, And

deem-ed thro' His infinite mer - cy, His child and forev - er I am.
know that the light of His presence With me doth continual - ly dwell.
sing, for I can- not be si - lent, His love is the theme of my song.
lov - ing-ly guardeth my footsteps, And giveth me songs in the night.
soon with the spir- its made per-fect, At home with the Lord I shall be.

REFRAIN.

Re - deemed, Re - deemed, Redeemed by the blood of the
Redeemed,   redeemed,

Lamb, Re - deemed. re - deemed, His child and forever I am.
Redeemed,   redeemed.

Copyright, 1882, by W. J. KIRKPATRICK.
30

No. 31. FROM DEATH UNTO LIFE.

ALICE CARY.　　　　　　　　　　W. J. KIRKPATRICK. By per.

1. Till I learned to love thy name, Lord, thy grace de - ny - ing,
2. Nothing could the world impart, Darkness held no mor - row;
3. When I learned to love thy name, O thou meek and low - ly;
4. Henceforth shall cre - a - tion ring With Sal - va - tion's sto - ry,

I was lost in sin and shame, Dying, Dy-ing, Dy - ing!
In my soul and in my heart, Sorrow, Sorrow, Sor - row!
Rap-ture kin - dled to a flame, Ho-ly, Ho - ly, Ho - ly!
Till I rise with thee to sing Glo-ry, Glo-ry, Glo - ry!

REFRAIN.

1 & 2. This is now my constant theme, This my favorite sto - ry.
3 & 4. Hal - le - lu - jah, grace is free, I will tell the sto - ry.

Je - sus' blood a - vails for me, Glo-ry, Glo-ry, Glo - ry!
Je - sus' blood hath made me free, Glo-ry, Glo-ry, Glo - ry!

No. 32. CHILD, YOUR FATHER CALLS.

(Dedicated to Chaplain McCabe.)

ANNIE M. STOCKTON.   REV. J. H. STOCKTON. By per.

1. Come home, dear sin-ner, while the light Is beam-ing on your way,
2. Come home, dear sin-ner; by the cross, Your Saviour waits for you;
3. Come home, dear sin-ner, while you feel The spir-it move your heart;
4. Come home, dear sin-ner, while you may, The church is call-ing too;
5. Come home, dear sin-ner, Je-sus' blood Can wash out ev-'ry stain;

The door stands o-pen wide for you, Re-turn while yet you may.
He'll cleanse a-way your earthly dross, And make you hap-py too.
While at the mer-cy seat you kneel, With ev-'ry i-dol part.
With ear-nest faith be-gin to pray, And heav'n will welcome you.
Plunge now in-to the crimson flood Of him who once was slain.

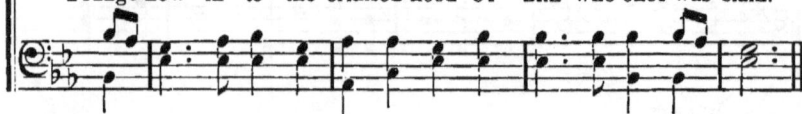

REFRAIN.

Come home, come home, dear child, come home, Your Father bids you come;

Come home, come home, just now come home, O wea-ry wand'rer come.

No. 33.   **"HEAVEN'S NICE."**

"O God! Heaven's nice—Thank you." Allie Roach, deceased.

Thos. E. Roach.   Jho. R. Sweney. By per.

1. I sing of Heav'n, that world of light Beyond the azure skies, Where
2. That Heaven must be "nice" indeed, No sor-row, pain, nor care, Nor
3. The Heav'nly cit-y I behold, In grand-eur bright and clear, With
4. There, shining ranks of an-gels stand, And children there I see— O,
5. Some day, on radiant wing, they'll come And bear me to the skies, To

nev-er comes the gloom of night, Where grand-est glo-ries rise.
death, shall cast a blighting shade, No sin can en-ter there.
pearl-y gates, and streets of gold, And walls of jew-els rare.
what a bright se-ra-phic band! When will they come for me?
join them in their hap-py home, And prove that "Heaven's nice,"

REFRAIN.

O, "Heaven's nice!" I know it is All beau-ti-ful and fair;— A

bright-er, bet-ter world than this, And I've a man-sion there.

33

DAILY VICTORY.

From the CHRISTIAN WOMAN.　　　　　　　　　　　JNO. R. SWENEY. By per.

Moderato.

1. I want a present living faith, That I may prove each day, each hour,
2. I want a firm, unwavering faith, That bringeth good from seeming ill;
3. I want a faith that falters not, Let skies be bright or tempest beat,

A - mid the toils and cares of life, My precious
That e'en a - mid af - flic - tion's blast, Re - joic - es
That 'mid earth's joys and cares and griefs, Vic - tor - ious

Sav - iour's love and power, *love and power;* I want a - mid the pet-ty
in the Father's will, *Father's will;* That when long-cherished hope's de-
sits at Je - sus' feet, *Jesus' feet;* Give me such faith, and then I

cares That dai - ly worry and an-noy, To live by faith so near my
nied, Still sings "a glad triumphant song," Knowing that He who reigns on
know When I shall pass cold Jordan's wave, The faith that kept me day by

God That life shall be.................. a constant joy, *constant joy.*
high— A God of love.................. can do no wrong, *do no wrong.*
day Will be triumph - - - - ant o'er the grave, *o'er the grave.*

From "Joy to the World."

DELIVERANCE WILL COME.

ANON. ANON.

1. I saw a way-worn trav'ler, In tat-ter'd garments clad,
His back was la-den heav-y, His strength was al-most gone,

And struggling up the mountain, It seemed that he was sad;
Yet he shout-ed as he journey'd, De-liv-erance will come.

REFRAIN.

Then palms of vic-to-ry, crowns of glo-ry, Palms of victo-ry I shall wear.

2. The summer sun was shining,
The sweat was on his brow,
His garments worn and dusty,
His step seemed very slow:
But he kept pressing onward,
For he was wending home;
Still shouting as he journeyed,
Deliverance will come!

3. The songsters in the arbor
That stood beside the way,
Attracted his attention,
Inviting his delay:
His watchword being "Onward!"
He stopped his ears and ran,
Still shouting as he journeyed,
Deliverance will come!

4. I saw him in the evening,
The sun was bending low,
He'd overtopped the mountain
And reached the vale below:

He saw the golden city,—
His everlasting home,—
And shouted loud, Hosanna,
Deliverance will come!

5. While gazing on that city,
Just o'er the narrow flood,
A band of holy angels
Came from the throne of God:
They bore him on their pinions
Safe o'er the dashing foam,
And joined him in his triumph,—
Deliverance has come!

6. I heard the song of triumph
They sang upon that shore,
Saying, Jesus has redeemed us
To suffer nevermore:
Then, casting his eyes backward
On the race which he had run,
He shouted loud, Hosanna,
Deliverance has come!

No. 36. BRINGING IN THE SHEAVES.

Words from "Songs of Glory."

Geo. A. Minor. By per.

1. Sowing in the morning, sowing seeds of kindness, Sowing in the noon-tide,
2. Sowing in the sunshine, sowing in the shadows, Fearing neither clouds nor
3. Go, then, ever weeping, sowing for the Master, Though the loss sustained our

and the dew-y eves; Waiting for the harvest, and the time of reap-ing,
winter's chilling breeze; By and by the harvest, and the la - bor en - ded,
spir- it oft-en grieves; When our weeping's over, He will bid us welcome,

REFRAIN.

We shall come re-joic-ing, bringing in the sheaves. Bringing in the sheaves,

bringing in the sheaves, We shall come rejoicing, bringing in the sheaves,

Bringing in the sheaves, bringing in the sheaves, We shall come rejoicing, bringing
[in the sheaves.

No. 37.   ERE THE SUN GOES DOWN.

Josephine Pollard.　　　　　　　　　　　　　W. J. Kirkpatrick. By per.

1. I have work enough to do Ere the sun goes down, For myself and kindred
2. I must speak the loving word Ere the sun goes down; I must let my voice be
3. As I journey on my way, Ere the sun goes down, God's commands I must o-

ere the sun goes down.

too, Ere the sun goes down. Ev'ry i-dle whisper stilling, With a
heard Ere the sun goes down; Ev'ry cry of pit-y heeding, For the
bey Ere the sun goes down. There are sins that need confessing, There are

ere the sun.

purpose firm and willing All my daily tasks fulfilling, Ere the sun goes down.
injured interceding, To the light the lost ones leading, Ere the sun goes down!
wrongs that need redressing, If I would obtain the blessing Ere the sun goes down.

ere the sun goes down.

REFRAIN.

Ere the sun goes down, Ere the sun goes down,

rit.

I must do my dai-ly du-ty Ere the sun goes down.

goes down.

WHOSOEVER.

James Nicholson.   Jno. R. Sweney. By per.

1. I praise the Lord that one like me, For mercy may to Jesus flee; He
2. I was to sin a wretched slave, But Jesus died my soul to save; He
3. I look by faith and see this word, Stamp'd with the blood of Christ, my Lord, He
4. I now believe He saves my soul, His precious blood hath made me whole; He

says, that who - so - ev - er will, May seek and find sal - vation still.

REFRAIN.

My saviour's promise faileth never; He counts me in the Whoso-ev - er.

From "Gems of Praise."

No. 39.   THE SONG OF TRIUMPH.

Sallie Smith.   Jno. R. Sweney. By per.

1. We've listed in the royal ranks, and girded on the sword, And girded on the
2. We've listed in the royal ranks of our redeemer King, Of our Redeemer
3. Yes, we shall conquer through His grace, and gain the promised land, And gain
   [the promised

THE SONG OF TRIUMPH. Concluded.

sword, and girded on the sword; And forth we march in ar-mor bright, Our
King, of our Redeemer King, And though the strife may fiercely rage His
land, and gain the promised land, Arrayed in robes of righteousness, with

banners wide unfurled, Led on by Him who conquered death, and triumph o'er
[the world.
praise we'll gladly sing. Who, out of all His faithful ones will more than con-
[querors bring.
palms in ev'ry hand; Yes, we shall conquer through His grace, and in His king-
[dom stand.

REFRAIN.

Rejoice, rejoice, rejoice, rejoice, His mighty shield is o'er us! He
Rejoice, rejoice, rejoice, rejoice, The foe shall fall before us! A

1
tells us not to fear He tells us not to fear;
glor'ous time is *Omit.*

2
coming soon, our victory is near.

’TIS WELL WITH ME.

F. J. C.   JNO. R. SWENEY. By per.

1, My hope has found an an-chor, A sure, a-bid-ing home,
2. I bless Thy word that taught me My lost es-tate to see;
3. ’Tis well where’er Thou lead-est, For Thou art with me still.

Up-on the Rock of A-ges, Where storms can nev-er come:
And since the hap-py mo-ment I gave my all to Thee,
’Tis well, whate’er Thou do-est, Be-cause my Sav-iour’s will:

And though I hear the tu-mult Of o-cean sur-ges swell.
The way I thought so drea-ry, With light and beau-ty glows,
And where my hope has anchored, There faith and love shall dwell;

My soul is calm and peaceful,—’Tis well with me, ’tis well.
And all a-long its windings A cool-ing foun-tain flows.
And what-so-e’er be-fall me, I’ll an-swer, Lord, ’tis well.

REFRAIN.

O Thou, whose blood has cleans’d me, My joy I can-not tell; But

'TIS WELL WITH ME. Concluded.

this my thankful heart can say,—'Tis well with me, 'tis well.

No. 41. JESUS SAVES ME ALL THE TIME.

JAMES NICHOLSON.   J. A. DUNCAN. By per.

1. Je - sus saves me ev - 'ry day; Je - sus saves me ev - 'ry night;
2. Je - sus saves, when I re - pine; Je - sus saves, when I re - joice;
3. Je - sus saves me, He is mine; Je - sus saves me, I am His;
4. Je - sus saves, He saves from sin, Je - sus saves, I feel Him nigh;

Je - sus saves me all the way—Thro' the dark - ness, thro' the light.
Je - sus saves, when hopes decline—Faith can al - ways hear His voice.
Je - sus saves, while I re - cline On His precious prom - is - es.
Je - sus saves, He dwells with - in, Glad - ly do I tes - ti - fy.

REFRAIN.

Je - sus saves, oh bliss sub - lime, Je - sus saves me all the time.

No. 42. SWEETLY I'M RESTING IN JESUS.

W. J. K.

W. J. KIRKPATRICK. By per.

1. Sweetly I'm rest-ing in Je - sus, Trusting my Saviour and Lord;
2. Sweetly I'm rest-ing in Je - sus, Plunged in the life-giving flood.
3. Sweetly I'm rest-ing in Je - sus, Glory-light beams on my way,
4. Sweetly I'm rest-ing in Je - sus, Safe on His bosom reclined;

Cast-ing my soul on His mer - cy, Lean-ing up - on His word;
Bathed in the sea of re-demp-tion, Washed in the cleans-ing blood;
Bright'ning my path through the darkness, Chasing the clouds a - way,
To-kens of per-fect sal - va - tion, Full-ness of joy I find,

Bear-ing the cross through toil and pain, Counting as loss all earthly gain;
Pas-sive-ly ly - ing at His feet, Learning the bliss of love complete;
Feed-ing in pas-tures green and fair, Drinking from fountains flowing there,
Pur - er and clear-er all the way, Shin-eth the light of per-fect day;

FINE.

Refrain on next page.

Knowing the faithful a crown shall obtain. Sweetly I'm resting in Je - sus.
Wait-ing His pleasure whatever is meet, Sweetly I'm resting in Je - sus.
Tenderly guarded by His loving care, Sweetly I'm resting in Je - sus.
Holy the rapture, triumphant the lay, Sweetly I'm resting in Je - sus.

D.S. Blessed assurance, His name be adored, Sweetly I'm resting in Je - sus.

42

SWEETLY I'M RESTING IN JESUS. Concluded.

REFRAIN.

D.S.

Sweet - ly rest - ing, Firm - ly trusting His word;
Sweet-ly I'm rest-ing in Je—sus my Lord, Firm-ly I'm trusting, be - lievingHis word;

No. 43.   GLORY TO HIS NAME!

E. A. HOFFMAN.

Rev. J. H. STOCKTON. By per.

[cried,

1. Down at the cross where the Saviour died, Down where for cleansing from sin I
2.   I am so wondrously saved from sin;   Je - sus so sweetly abides within,
3. O precious fountain, that saves from sin, I am so glad I have entered in;
4. Come to this fountain, so rich and sweet; Humble your soul at the Saviour's feet;

FINE.

There to my heart was the blood applied, Glo - ry to His name!
There at   the cross where He took me in, Glo - ry to His name!
There Je - sus saves me, and keeps me clean, Glo - ry to His name!
Plunge in   to-day, and be made complete, Glo - ry to His name!

.D. S. There to my heart was the blood applied, Glo - ry to His name!

REFRAIN.

D. S.

Glo-ry to His   name!   Glo-ry to His name!

No. 44. JESUS WILL GIVE YOU REST.

FANNY J. CROSBY.　　　　　　　　　　　JNO. R. SWENEY. BY per.

1. Will you come, will you come, with your poor broken heart, Burden'd and sin-op-
2. Will you come, will you come? there is mercy for you, Balm for your aching
3. Will you come, will you come, you have nothing to pay; Jesus who loves you
4. Will you come, will you come? how he pleads with you now! Fly to His loving

pressed?　Lay it down at the feet of your Sa - viour and Lord,
breast;　On - ly come as you are, and be-lieve on his name,
best.　By his death on the Cross pur-chased life for your soul,
breast;　And what-ev - er your sin or your sor - row may be,

REFRAIN.

Je - sus will give you rest.　O happy rest, sweet, happy rest!

Je - sus will give you rest.　hap-py rest.　Oh! why won't you come in

sim - ple, trust - ing faith? Je - sus will give you rest.

From "Joy to the World."

No. 45. GATHER THE REAPERS HOME.

JENNIE JOHNSON.　　　　　　　　　　　　　JNO. R. SWENEY. By per.

1. Have ye heard the song from the golden land? Have ye heard the glad new
2. They are look- ing down from the golden land, Our beloved are look- ing
3. O the song rolls　on from the golden land, And our hearts are strong to-
4. O the song rolls　on from the golden land, From its vales of joy and

song, Let us bind our sheaves with a willing hand, For the time will not be long.
down, They have done their work, they have borne their cross, And received their
　　　　　　　　　　　　　　　　　　　　　　　　　　　[promised crown.
day, For it nerves our souls with its music sweet, And we toil in the noon-tide ray.
flowers, And we feel and know by a living faith That its tones will soon be ours.

REFRAIN.

The Lord of the har - vest will soon ap - pear, His

smile, His voice we shall see and hear, The Lord of the harvest will

soon ap - pear And gath - er the reap - ers home.

45

No. 46. 'TIS SO SWEET TO TRUST IN JESUS.

Mrs. Louisa M. R. Stead.   W. J. Kirkpatrick.   By per.

1. 'Tis so sweet to trust in   Je - sus, Just to take Him at His Word;
2. O, how sweet to trust in   Je - sus, Just to trust His cleansing blood;
3. Yes, 'tis sweet to trust in   Je - sus, Just from sin and self to cease;
4. I'm so glad I learn'ed to trust Thee, Precious Je - sus, Saviour, Friend

Just to rest up - on his promise; Just to know, "Thus saith the Lord."
Just in sim - ple faith to plunge me 'Neath the healing, cleansing flood
Just from Je - sus sim-ply tak - ing Life, and rest, and joy, and peace.
And I know that thou art with me, Wilt be with me to the end.

REFRAIN.

Je - sus, Je - sus, how I trust him; How I've prov'd him o'er and o'er.

Je - sus, Je - sus, Precious Je - sus! O for grace to trust him more.

No. 47. BEAUTIFUL DAY.

W. J. K.

W. J. KIRKPATRICK. By per.

1. Beau-ti-ful day, love-ly thy light; Holy each ray, nothing like night;
2. Beau-ti-ful day, calm was thy dawn; Joyous the lay, blessed the morn,
3. Beau-ti-ful day, per-fect-ly bright; Jesus alway, boundless delight.
4. Beau-ti-ful day, ha-ven of rest; Ev'ry one may come and be blest;

Cloudless thy sky; peaceful my stay Here in the sunlight of beautiful day.
When in my heart, over my way, First shone the noontide of beautiful day.
Bliss all around, heav'n by the way, Shining in fullness, oh, beautiful day.
Glory to God, naught can dismay; Christ is the light of this beautiful day.

REFRAIN.

Beautiful, beautiful day,
Beau-ti-ful, beau-ti-ful day,
Evermore shine on my way,
Evermore shine on my way,

Saviour, I pray, keep me alway, Safe in this beau-ti-ful day.
Beautiful day.

From "Leaflet Gems. No. 1."

No. 48. FILL ME NOW.

REV. E. H. STOKES, D. D.　　　　　　　　　　　　JNO. R. SWENEY. By per.

1. Hov - er o'er me, Ho - ly Spir- it; Bathe my trembling heart and brow;
2. Thou can'st fill me, gracious Spir- it, Tho' I can- not tell Thee how;
3. I am weakness, full of weakness; At Thy sa - cred feet I bow;
4. Cleanse and comfort; bless and save me; Bathe, oh, bathe my heart and brow;

Fill me with Thy hal- low'd presence, Come, oh, come and fill me now.
But I need Thee, great-ly need Thee, Come, oh, come and fill me now.
Blest, di - vine, e - ter - nal Spir - it, Fill with pow-er, and fill me now.
Thou art com- fort- ing and sav - ing, Thou art sweet- ly fill- ing now.

Fine.

D.S. Fill me with Thy hal-low'd presence,—Come, oh, come and fill me now.

REFRAIN.　　　　　　　　　　　　　　　　　　　　D.S.

Fill me now, fill me now, Je - sus, come and fill me now

No. 49. FIRM TO THE END.

JENNIE JOHNSON.　　　　　　　　　　　　JNO. R. SWENEY. By per.

1. We are banded to-geth-er for Jes- us still to live, And to
2. We are marching to-geth er a - long the bless-ed way, Our Re-
3. We are marching to-geth-er, sore con-flicts we shall meet, But the
4. We are marching to-geth-er be - yond these fad- ing skies, We are

FIRM TO THE END. Concluded.

:S:

fol- low wherever he may lead; And the grace He has promised we
deem-er commandeth us to go; With the cloud and the pil - lar to
Saviour beholds us from his throne; With the sword of the Spir- it temp-
looking beyond the billows foam; We are wait- ing and watching with

D.S. tried and the faithful who

Fine.

know that He will give, If be - liev- ing, His precious name we plead.
lead us night and day, While beside us the liv - ing wa - ters flow.
ta - tions we'll de-feat, Our pro- tect - or will leave us not a - lone.
calm and trus- ty eyes, Till the Saviour shall come and call us home.

serve the mas- ter here, Shall be Jewels to sparkle in His crown.

REFRAIN.

Then be firm to the end, then be firm to the end; Let us

D.S.

never, never lay our ar - mor down, For the
Ar - mor down.

COMING TO JESUS.

REV. W. H. BURRELL.

JNO. R. SWENEY. By per.

1. With my sin-wounded soul, To be made ful - ly whole, And Thy
2. Oh, how long I have tried To re - sist na - ture's tide! All in
3. I, Thy prom-ise be- lieve That in Thee I shall live, Thro' Thy
4. To be Thine, wholly thine, Precious Sav-iour di - vine, With my

per - fect sal - va - tion to see, With my heart all a - glow, To be
vain have I sighed to be free; In my-self all undone, 'Neath the
blood shed so free - ly for me; To ob- tain a pure heart, And se-
all con - se - crat- ed to Thee; To be kept ev -'ry hour, By Thy

wash'd white as snow, I am com - ing, dear Sav- iour, to Thee.
waves sink-ing down, I am com - ing, dear Sav- iour, to Thee.
cure the good part, I am com - ing, dear Sav- iour, to Thee.
love's wondrous power, I am com - ing, dear Sav- iour, to Thee.

REFRAIN.

I am coming, dear Saviour, to Thee, I am coming, dear Saviour, to Thee, With my

heart all a-glow, To be wash'd white as snow, I am coming, dear Saviour, to Thee.

SAVED TO THE UTTERMOST.

W. J. K.   W. J. KIRKPATRICK. By per.

1. Saved to the ut - termost: I am the Lord's, Je - sus, my Saviour, sal-
2. Saved to the ut - termost: Je - sus is near, Keeping me safe - ly, he
3. Saved to the ut - termost: this I can say, "Once all was darkness, but
4. Saved to the ut - termost: cheerful-ly sing Loud hal - le - lu - ias to

va - tion af-fords. Gives me His Spir - it a wit - ness, with - in,
cast-eth out fear, Trusting His prom - is - es, how I am blest
now it is day," Beau-ti - ful vis - ions of glo - ry I see,
Je - sus, my King, Ransom'd and par - don'd, re-deem'd by His blood.

REFRAIN.

Whisp'ring of par - don, and sav - ing from sin. Saved, saved,
Lean-ing up - on him, how sweet is my rest.
Je - sus in brightness re - vealed un - to me.
Cleans'd from un-right-eous-ness, glo - ry to God.

saved to the ut-termost; Saved, saved, by power divine; Saved, saved, I'm

saved to the ut - termost, Je - sus, the Sa-viour, is mine.

From " Precious Songs."

No. 52. IS NOT THIS THE LAND OF BEULAH?

ANON.   ARRANGED.

1. I am dwelling on the mountain, Where the golden sun-light gleams
2. I can see far down the mountain, Where I wandered wea-ry years,
3. I am drinking at the fountain, Where I ev - er would a-bide;
4. Tell me not of heav-y cross-es, Nor the bur-dens hard to bear,
5. Oh! the Cross has wondrous glory! Oft I've proved this to be true;

O'er a land whose wondrous beauty Far exceeds my fond-est dreams;
Oft - en hin - dered in my jour-ney, By the ghosts of doubts and fears,
For I've tast - ed life's pure riv - er, And my soul is sat - is - fied;
For I've found this great sal-va - tion Makes each burden light ap-pear;
When I'm in the way so nar-row I can see a path-way through

Where the air is pure, e-the-real, La-den with the breath of flowers
Brok-en vows and dis-appointments Thickly sprinkled all the way,
There's no thirst-ing for life's pleasures, Nor a-dorn-ing, rich and gay,
And I love to fol-low Je - sus, Glad-ly counting all but dross,
And how sweet-ly Je-sus whispers: Take the Cross, thou need'st not fear,

CHO. Is not this the land of Beu-lah, Bless-ed, bless-ed land of light,

D.S. for Chorus.

That are bloom-ing by the fountain, 'Neath the am - a - ranthine bowers.
But the Spir - it led un - er-ring To the land I hold to day.
For I've found a rich-er treas-ure, One that fad-eth not a - way.
World-ly hon - ors all for-sak-ing For the glo - ry of the Cross.
For I've tried this way be-fore thee, And the glo-ry lin - gers near.

Where the flow - ers bloom for ev - er, And the sun is al- ways bright.

52

TOILING UP THE WAY.

Arr. by Jno. R. Sweney. By per.

Moderato.

1. We are toil-ing up the way, Nar-row way, narrow way; We have
2. Though the journey may be long, Hard and long, hard and long, We will
3. We shall gath-er home at last, Sor-row past, sor-row past; We shall
4. We shall know each oth-er there, O-ver there, o-ver there, When our

journey'd many a day T'ward the kingdom: T'ward the distant shining land, [Golden
cheer it with a song Of the kingdom; We shall en-ter by the cross, Blessed
hold our jewels fast In the kingdom; We shall dwell in perfect light, Holy
angel robes we wear, In the kingdom; All that's purest, holi'est here, Grows more

D.S. And the shining angels wait, angels

FINE.

land, gold-en land, Where the heav'nly harpers stand In the king-dom.
cross, blessed cross; Gaining gold that hath no dross, In the king-dom.
light, ho-ly light, Never dimm'd by tears at night, In the king-dom.
dear, grows more dear, In the mansions drawing near, In the king-dom.

wait, an-gels wait, To un-bar the golden gate Of the king-dom.

REFRAIN.

D.S.

Still we sing, Christ, our King, Walks with us the wea-ry way.

COMING BY AND BY.

R. L.

R. Lowry. By per.

1. A better day is coming, A morning promised long, When girded Right, with
2. The boast of haughty Error No more will fill the air, But Age and Youth will
3. Oh! for that holy dawning We watch, and wait, and pray, Till o'er the height the

holy Might, Will o'erthrow the Wrong; When God the Lord will listen To
love the Truth, And spread it ev'rywhere; No more from Want and Sorrow Will
morning light Shall drive the gloom away; And when the heav'nly glory Shall

ev'ry plaintive sigh, And stretch his hand o'er ev'ry land, With justice by and by.
come the hopeless cry; And strife will cease, and perfect Peace Will flourish by and
[by.
flood the earth and sky, We'll bless the Lord for all His word, And praise Him by
[and by.

REFRAIN.

Com-ing by and by, com-ing by and by! The bet-ter day is
Com-ing by and by, com-ing by and by! The wel-come dawn will

coming, The morning draweth nigh;
(Omit.)
has-ten on,'Tis coming by and by.

No. 55. THE LORD IS MY LIGHT.

JAMES NICHOLSON.   JNO. R. SWENEY. By per.

1. The Lord is my light, then why should I fear, By day and by night His
2. The Lord is my light, the Lord is my strength, I know in His might I'll
3. The Lord is my light, my all and in all, There is in 'His sight no

presence is near; He is my sal-va-tion from sor-row and sin, This
conquer at length; My weakness in mer-cy he cov-ers with pow'r, And
darkness at all; He is my Redeemer, my Saviour and King, With

REFRAIN.

blessed as - surance the Spir-it doth bring. The Lord   is my
walking by faith I am saved ev-'ry hour.
saints and with angels His praises I sing. The Lord is   my light, The

light,   He is my joy,   and my song,   By
Lord   is   my light,   He is   my joy,   and   my song, By

day   and by night,   He leads, He leads me along.
day and by night, by   day   and by night.

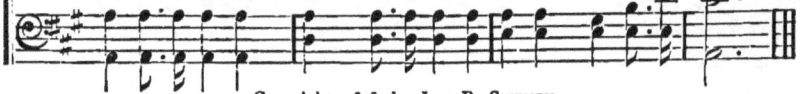

55

No. 56. THOU KNOWEST THAT I LOVE THEE.

JAMES NICHOLSON.   W. J. KIRKPATRICK. By per.

1. Je - sus, my precious Sav-iour, Though I have oft - en erred, And
2. In times of sore temp-ta - tion; Oh bit - ter, bit - ter thought! Like
3. Still in Thy ten-der mer - cy, Thou dost to me ex-tend The
4. I feel the warm out-gushing, Of Thy great love for me, And

REFRAIN.

grieved Thy Holy Spir-it In thought, and word, and deed. Thou knowest that I
Pe - ter I was faithless, As if I knew Thee not.
scep-tre of Thy fa - vor, And treat me as a friend.
Lord! "Thou knowest all things" Thou knowest I love Thee.

love Thee, My Saviour, ev-er kind, Thou knowest that I love Thee, With

heart, and soul, and mind. I love Thee,   I love Thee, And sweet peace I find.
                        o yes,   my saviour

No. 57.   SAVE ME NOW.

FANNY J. CROSBY.   W. J. KIRKPATRICK. By per.

1. Sin-ner, would thou find a ref-uge? Come to Je-sus as thou
2. He has called, and knocked and waited, But thy soul re-fused to
3. Sin-ner, these are gold-en moments, Kind-ly lent thee to im-
4. If His con-stant ad-mo-ni-tions Thou con-tin-ue to re-

art, In the blood of His a-tonement, Ask of Him to cleanse thy heart.
bow; Once a-gain His spir-it warns thee, Haste and bid Him en-ter now.
plore, Slight no more the gospel message, Grieve no more a Saviour's love.
fuse, Death perchance may overtake thee, Then 'twill be too late to choose.

REFRAIN.

Save me now, save me now, Let thy soul's pe-ti-tion be: If that

prayer in faith is off-er'd He will hear and an-swer thee.

THE KINGDOM IS COMING.

Words Adapted by G. E. L.

Jno. R. Sweney. By per

1. In all the bright fac - es of earth's heav'n-ly plac - es, Be-
2. From the bright crys-tal fountains Of God's Ho - ly mountains, O
3. With the Lamb on the throne, in the midst of His own, By the

hold how the Spir- it doth shine,
see how the pure wa-ters flow.
banks of Life's riv - er we'll stand.

Our Lord doth pos- sess them, His
The des - erts are blooming, The
Re-deemed from de-struction, To

FINE.

pres - ence doth bless them, They're filled with the Spirit di - vine.
earth they're per - fum- ing, The na - tions their Sav - iour do know.
sing res - ur - rec- tion, A sin - conqu'ring, glo - ri - fied band.

D.S. knowl-edge and glo - ry, As wa - ters that cov - er the sea.

The King-dom is com - ing, Go tell ye the sto - ry, God's

D.S.

ban - ner ex - alt - ed we see. The earth He doth fill With His

Copyright, 1882, by Jno. R. Sweney.

No. 59. IS MY NAME WRITTEN THERE?

M. A. K.   FRANK M. DAVIS. By per.

1. Lord, I care not for rich-es, Neither silver nor gold, I would make sure of
2. Lord, my sins they are many, Like the sands of the sea, But Thy blood, Oh, my
3. Oh! that beau-ti-ful cit - y, With its mansions of light, With its glorified

heaven, I would en - ter the fold. In the book of Thy kingdom, With its
Sav-iour! Is suf - fi - cient for me; For Thy promise is written In bright
be - ings, In pure garments of white, Where no e - vil thing cometh, To de-

pa - ges so fair, Tell me, Je - sus, my Saviour, Is my name written there?
letters that glow, "Though your sins be as scarlet, I will make them like snow."
spoil what is fair; Where the angels are watching, Is my name written there?

REFRAIN.

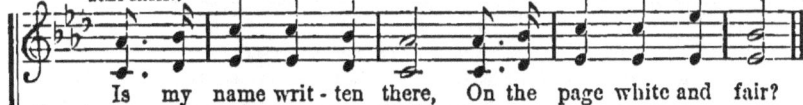

Is my name writ - ten there, On the page white and fair?

In the book of Thy king - dom, Is my name writ-ten there?

No. 60. BEAUTIFUL CANAAN ABOVE.

FRANK GOULD.   JNO. R. SWENEY. By per.

1. In the Canaan that lies o-ver Jor - dan, In the beauti- ful Canaan a-
2. In the Canaan that lies o-ver Jor - dan, In the Canaan of promise so
3. We are drifting along to the Jor - dan, And we list to its swift rolling
4. O the Canaan that lies o-ver Jordan, What a greeting of joy there will

bove, We are go - ing to dwell, and for - ev - er, With
fair; Where the vines with their clusters are bend - ing, We shall
tide, But we know for the Saviour has told us That His
be When we join the glad cho- rus e - ter - nal, And the

REFRAIN.

Je - sus to feast on His love. Where the verdure of spring is im-
rest from our la - bor and care.
staff shall the wa - ters di - vide.
walls of Mount Zi - on we see.

mor - tal, And the leaves nev- er fade nor de - cay, Where the

win - ter of age can - not en - ter, And the years never cir - cle a - way.

I'M SAVED.

REV. E. H. STOKES, D. D.   JNO. A. DUNCAN. By per.

1. I'm saved! I'm saved! oh, blessed Lord, I'm sweet-ly saved in
2. I'm saved, I'm saved! oh, joy sub-lime! I'm saved from self and
3. Saved at the cross, the blessed cross, Saved without and with-
4. I'm saved, I'm saved, I'll tell it here, I'll sing it o'er and

Thee,   Saved by Thy blood and by Thy word, And
sin,   I'm saved, I'm saved, oh, bliss di - vine! And
in,   I'm saved, I'm saved, oh, what a loss Who
o'er;   I'm saved in Je - sus, oh, how sweet! I'll

REFRAIN.

thine henceforth will be.   I'm saved! I'm saved! I'm
love has closed me in.
fail this joy to win.
sing it ev - er - more.

saved!   I'm washed in the blood of the Lamb,   I'm

saved! I'm saved! I'm saved!   I'm washed in the blood of the Lamb.

No. 62.   GOING HOME.

Miss P. J. Owens.

W. J. Kirkpatrick. By per.

[stretched to

1. O, detain me not, ye many loved ones clinging, There are dearer hands out-
2. I have wander'd long, a weary stranger, sighing For the peaceful meadows on that
3. Do not keep me here while all my heart is yearning For the holy rapture of that

welcome me, Where the joy-ous angels' harps are sweetly ringing; 'Tis my
ver-nal shore; I am go-ing home to where there is no dy-ing, For my
sin-less home, Let me has-ten on, their welcome song returning, Flutt'ring

REFRAIN.

Saviour calls, I may not stay with thee. Heav'nly home, heav'nly home, O how
Saviour gives me life forevermore.
pulses cease, for endless life is come.

Heav'nly home, past the billows' foam,

sweet your rest will be;   Fleeting earth-ly years, flowing
O how sweet

rall.

fare-well tears, Je-sus waits   to welcome me.
waits to welcome me,   Je-sus waits to welcome me.

No.63. LO, THE GOLDEN FIELDS ARE SMILING.

FANNY J. CROSBY.   W. J. KIRKPATRICK. By per.

1. Lo, the golden fields are smil-ing, Wherefore i-dle shouldst thou be?
2. Take the balm of con-so-la-tion, That so oft has cheered thy heart;
3. Go and gather souls for Je-sus, Preci-ous souls thy love may win;
4. Go then work, the Master call-eth, Go, no longer i-dle be;

Great the harvest, few the workers, And the Lord hath need of thee.
Let some weary brother toil-er, In thy comfort share a part.
Lead them to the door of mer-cy, Tell them how to en-ter in,
Waste no more thy precious moments, For the Lord hath need of thee.

Go and work, the time is wan-ing, Let thy earnest heart reply
Go and lift the heavy bur-den, He has struggled long to bear,
Go and gath-er souls for Jesus, Work while strength and breath remain,
Once He gave His life thy ran-som, That thy soul with Him might live,

:S: ad lib.   FINE.

To the call so oft re-peat-ed, "Bless-ed Master, here am I."
Go, and kneeling down beside him, Blend thy faith with his in prayer.
What are years of con-stant la-bor, To the joy thou yet shalt gain.
Now the ser-vice he de-mand-eth, Can thy heart refuse to give?

D.S. Go and fill thy place among them, For the Lord hath need of thee.

REFRAIN.   D.S.

Hark, the song, the song of busy workers, In the fields so fair to see;

No. 64. JESUS MY SOUL'S REDEEMER.

FANNY ANDERSON.   JNO. R. SWENEY. By per.

1. What have I done, O Lord, for Thee? Yet Thou hast done great things for me:
2. What have I done Thy cause to spread? Yet, for my sins Thy heart has bled;
3. What have I done to serve Thee here? What have I done, sad hearts to cheer?
4.   O, let my heart and hand u - nite, Scattering seed with early light,

FINE.

Thou from the law hast made me free, Je - sus, my soul's Redeem - er.
Yes, on the cross Thy blood was shed, Jesus, my soul's Redeem - er.
Yet, Thou hast borne my ev - 'ry fear, Je - sus, my soul's Redeem - er.
Working for Thee from morn till night Je-sus, my soul's Redeem - er.

D. S. Firm on the Rock I stand to-day, Je - sus my soul's Redeem - er.

REFRAIN.   *D.S.*

Out of the deep and mi - ry clay Lo, Thou hast taken my feet away,

Copyright, 1882, by JNO. R. SWENEY.

No. 65. JESUS, MY SAVIOUR, LOVES ME.

FANNY J. CROSBY.   JNO. R. SWENEY. By per.

1. Je - sus has brought me from darkness to light, Now I am singing from
2. Once I was lone-ly and sorrow oppressed, Once I was wear-y and
3. Once I was thoughtless but now I believe, Nev-er my Saviour, a-

Copyright, 1882, by JNO. R. SWENEY.

64

JESUS, MY SAVIOUR, LOVES ME. Concluded.

morn-ing till night, Sing-ing, as hap-py as mor-tal can be,
long-ing for rest, Now from the bondage of sin I am free
gain will I grieve; Clos-er, and clos-er to Him would I be,

Je-sus, my Saviour, loves me! Let me proclaim it to all that I meet,
Je-sus, my Saviour, loves me! Since, my forgiveness, He tender-ly spoke,
Je-sus, my Saviour, loves me! Out in the sunshine of mer-cy di-vine,

Let me proclaim it, the story is sweet, Jesus has suffered that I might be free,
Light is my burden and easy my yoke; Now in His service what beauty I see,
O, what a fulness of rapture is mine, This my rejoicing, my boasting shall be,

REFRAIN.

Je-sus, my Saviour, loves me! Glo-ry! glo-ry! Jesus, my Saviour, loves

me, loves me! Glo-ry! glo-ry! My Saviour, my Saviour loves me!

Copyright, 1882, by Jno. R. Sweney.

No. 66. LET ME CLING TO THEE.

Rev. Edwin H. Nevin, D.D.

W. J. Kirkpatrick. By per.

1. O, let me cling to Thee, My Saviour, Let me cling to Thee! When the
2. O, let me cling to Thee, My Saviour, Let me cling to Thee! When my
3. O, let me cling to Thee, My Saviour, Let me cling to Thee! When my
4. O, let me cling to Thee, My Saviour, Let me cling to Thee! When I'm

winds are blowing, When the tears are flowing, O, let me cling to Thee!
friends are leaving, When my heart is grieving, O, let me cling to Thee!
sins are pressing, And my soul distressing, O, let me cling to Thee!
weak and weary, And my path is dreary, O, let me cling to Thee!

REFRAIN.

Let me ev - er cling to Thee, Let me ev - er cling to Thee! Let me
my Saviour, Let me

cling, Let me cling, O, Saviour, let me cling to Thee!
cling with faith in pray'r, And with hope amid despair. to Thee!

5. O, let me cling to Thee,
    My Saviour,
Let me cling to Thee!
    When the cloud is o'er me,
    And the storm before me,
O, let me cling to Thee!

6. O, let me cling to Thee,
    My Saviour,
Let me cling to Thee!
    When I cross the river,
    Which from earth doth sever,
O, let me cling to Thee!

No. 67. CHRIST MY LORD.

Mrs. H. E. Brown.   W. J. Kirkpatrick. By per.

1. O Thou Unseen, but pre - sent Christ, My loved and lov - ing Lord;
2. Thou art the source of all the life, That in my life I see;
3. Thou art the pearl of greatest price, My tru - est no - blest wealth;
4. Thou art my suc - cor in distress, My guard, be - hind, be - fore;
5. Whom have I, Lord, in Heav'n but Thee? And who in earth be - side?

Thou art the Friend a -bove all friends, With- in my heart a - dored.
The fountain of my faith and hope; My springs are all in Thee.
Thou the indwell - ing quick- en - er, My soul's e - ter - nal health.
My shield from fier - y darts of sin, My help for- ev - er - more.
With-in Thy heart Thou holdest me, In mine Thou dost a - bide.

REFRAIN.

Praises high, and praises ho - ly, Loud and long I sing.

Hal - le - lu - jah, hal - le - lu - jah, Un - to Christ my King.

No. 68. THERE IS ROOM FOR THEE.

LIZZIE EDWARDS.   JNO. R. SWENEY. By per.

1. I came to God and my soul was lost, I stood on the brink of woe,
2. I came to God and my sins confessed, My sins that I could not bear;
3. I came to God and He made me clean, I plunged in the healing wave;
4. I came to God in a child-like faith, A faith that has made me whole;

FINE.

I knew and felt that His arm would save, To Him I a-lone must go.
I knelt me down with a brok-en heart, I prayed, and he heard my prayer.
He bade me look at the cross He bore, And life for a look He gave.
A joy is mine that the world knows not, The joy of a new born soul.

D.S. wand'rer come to His arms of love, O come, there is room for thee.

REFRAIN.   D.S.

And now a child of redeeming grace, I sing of His mercy free. O,

No. 69. THY HOPE FOR ETERNITY.

FANNY J. CROSBY.   JNO. R. SWENEY. By per.

1. O, what is thy hope for the fu - ture, And what of thy-self canst thou
2. O, what is thy hope for the future? 'Tis time thou should'st think of thy
3. Say, what is thy hope for the fu - ture, And where is thy hav - en? O

THY HOPE FOR ETERNITY. Concluded.

say? Art thou coming repentant to Je - sus, Or grieving the Spirit a
soul, When the moments like arrows are flying, And the years, oh, how swiftly they
where? Art thou nearing the harbor of glo - ry, Or nearing the brink of dis-

way? Art thou building a house that will perish, Or one that for-ever will
roll. Art thou storing the lessons of wisdom, So patiently taught by thy
pair? While the Saviour still waits to be gracious, Make haste, and His pardon im-

stand? Remember the fate of the foolish man That trusted the sinking sand.
Lord? Or carelessly treading beneath thy feet The pearls of His precious word.
plore; Make haste, or the mercy that warns thee now, Will plead with thy soul no
[more.

REFRAIN.

The blood of the cru - ci fied Sav - iour Was shed on the cross for

thee, But what is thy hope for the future, Thy hope for eterni-ty?

Copyright, 1882, by Jno. R. Sweney.
69

No. 70.   'TIS IMMANUEL'S LAND.

Fanny J. Crosby.   W. J. Kirkpatrick. By per.

Allegretto.

1. There's a land that for a-ges has stood, And for a-ges e-ternal shall
2. There's a land where the Spring never fades, And the skies are unclouded and
3. There's a land where the armies of God, Shalt return when their warfare is
4. There's a land that is perfect and pure, And our faith flies away to its
5. In that land where all storms are at rest, May we meet when our journey shall

stand; 'Tis the seat of the kingdom and throne of our Lord, And its
bright; Where the sower and reaper for - ev - er a - bide In its
done; Where the cross they have borne, shall be changed for a crown, And the
shore; Where the weary are safe in the arms of their Lord, And they
cease; There to tell the old stor - y, so dear to us now, By the

Refrain.

name is Imman - u - el's land.   'Tis Im - man - u - el's land, Im -
sweet happy vales of de - light.
righteous shall shine as the sun.
hunger and thirst nev - er - more.
clear flowing riv - er of peace.

man - u - el's land, The home of the saints far a - bove; There to

Jesus their King, Hallelujahs they sing; By the ocean of in - fi - nite love.

No. 71. I AM PERSUADED.

GRACIE E. LOVELIGHT.   W. J. KIRKPATRICK. By per.

1. I am persuaded, Now I be - lieve;   I am persuad - ed,
2. I am persuaded, Trusting His word;   Firmly I'm standing,
3. I am persuaded, Thine, Lord, to be;   Now and for-ev - er,
4. Lord, for Thy goodness, Thee I a - dore;   Anthems of rapt - ure,

Christ I re - ceive;   My soul can gladly say, Je - sus is
Strong in the Lord;   No more by sin oppressed, My soul doth
Walk ing with Thee;   Life, death nor an - y-thing Earth, heav'n, or
Up - ward shall soar;   To God the Father, Son, And Spir - it

mine to-day,   My hope, my guide, my stay, My all in all.
sweetly rest,   On my Redeemer's breast, Glo - ry to God!
hell can bring, Can part us while I cling, Sav - iour, to Thee.
Three in One, Let praise on earth begun, Ring ev - er - more.

No. 72. JESUS HEARS ME.

FANNY J. CROSBY.

JNO. R. SWENEY. By per.

1. I'll   praise, I'll praise the name of Je - sus, The name I breathe in
2. I'll   praise, I'll praise the name of Je - sus, His name my boast shall
3. I'll   praise, I'll praise the name of Je - sus, With ev - 'ry fleet- ing
4. I'll   praise, I'll praise the name of Je - sus, While time its flight shall

prayer,   It   draws me upward to the Fath- er's throne, And
be,   My   all I cheerful - ly to Him re - sign, No
breath,   I'll   praise and glo - ri - fy re - deem- ing grace, That
wing,   Then through the a - ges of e - ter - ni - ty, His

REFRAIN.

stills each throb of care.   Je - sus hears me, Je - sus saves me, I am
Friend so dear as He.
brought my soul from death.
bound- less love I'll sing.

quicken - ed   by   His cleans - ing power,   And

O how ten-der - ly He leads me on, And keeps me hour by hour;

GOING HOME TO GLORY.

R. K. C.

R. KELSO CARTER. By per.

1. O, sin-ner, come a-long with me, I'm go-ing home to glo-ry;
2. The world can charm my soul no more, I'm go-ing home to glo-ry;
3. I've left my sins behind the cross, I'm go-ing home to glo-ry;
4. I'm ransomed from the fearful fall, I'm go-ing home to glo-ry;

The blood of Je-sus sets you free, I'm go-ing home to glo-ry.
I'm bound to reach the heavenly shore, I'm go-ing home to glo-ry.
All earthly things I count but loss, I'm go-ing home to glo-ry.
And Je-sus is my all in all, I'm go-ing home to glo-ry.

REFRAIN.

I'm going home, I'm go-ing home, I'm go-ing
I'm go-ing home, I'm go-ing home,

home to die no more, I'm going home to glory; I'm going home, I'm going
I'm go-ing home,

home, I'm going home to die no more, I'm going home to glory.
I'm go-ing home,

No. 98   WILT THOU BE MADE WHOLE?

W. J. K.

W. J. KIRKPATRICK. By per.

1. Hear the foot-steps of Jesus, He is now passing by, Bearing balm for the
2. 'Tis the voice of that Saviour, Whose merci-ful call Free-ly off-ers sal-
3. Are you halting and struggling, O'er pow'red by your sin, While the waters are
4. Bless-ed Sav-iour as-sist us To rest on Thy word; Let the soul-healing

wounded, Healing all who ap-ply. As he spake to the suff'rer Who
va-tion To one and to all; He is now beck'ning to Him Each
troubled Can you not en-ter in? Lo the Sav-iour stands waiting To
pow-er On us now be out-poured: Wash away ev-'ry sin spot, Take

lay at the pool, He is say-ing this moment, "Wilt thou be made whole."
sin tainted soul, And lov-ing-ly ask-ing, "Wilt thou be made whole."
strengthen your soul, He is earnest-ly pleading, "Wilt thou be made whole."
per-fect con-trol, Say to each trusting spirit, "Thy faith makes thee whole."

REFRAIN.

Wilt thou be made whole? Wilt thou be made whole? O come wea-ry

suff'rer, O, come sin sick soul, See the life-stream is flow-ing, See the

WILT THOU BE MADE WHOLE? Concluded.

cleansing waves roll, Step in - to the cur-rent and thou shalt be whole.

No. 99.   JESUS COMES.

MRS. PHOEBE PALMER.   W. J. KIRKPATRICK.   By per.

1. Watch, ye saints, with eyelids waking Lo! the pow'rs of heav'n are shaking,
2. Lo! the prom - ise of your Sav-iour, Pardoned sin and purchased favor,
3. Kingdoms at their base are crumbling, Hark! His chariot wheels are rumbling,
4. Nations wane, though proud and stately, Christ His kingdom hasteneth greatly,

Keep your lamps all trimmed and burning, Ready for your Lord's re-turn-ing.
Blood-washed robes and crowns of glory; Haste to tell Redemption's sto - ry.
Tell, O, tell of grace abounding, While the seventh trump is sounding.
Earth her latest pangs is summing, Shout, ye saints, your Lord is coming.

REFRAIN. Lo! He comes, He comes all glorious, Je - sus comes to reign vic-to-rious,

Repeat Refrain.

Lo! He comes, Lo! Je - sus comes.

Lo! He comes. (*Omit.*)   Yes   Je - sus comes.

5.	6.
Lamb of God!—Thou meek and lowly,	Sinners, come, while Christ is pleading,
Judah's Lion!—High and Holy, [thee,"	Now for you He's interceding;
Lo! Thy "Bride comes forth to meet	Haste, ere grace and time diminished
All in blood-washed robes to greet thee.	Shall proclaim the mystery finished.

No. 100. TELLING THE STORY OF JESUS.

SALLIE SMITH. JNO. R. SWENEY. By per.

1. Strangers and pilgrims, we journey below, Telling the story of Je - sus;
2. Strangers and pilgrims, O, happy are we! Telling the story of Je - sus;
3. Strangers and pilgrims, yet looking above, Telling the story of Je - sus;
4. Strangers and pilgrims, yet soon we shall meet, Telling the story of Jesus;

Fearless and faithful to Zi - on we go, Telling the sto - ry of Je - sus.
Pleading with sinners His children to be, Telling the sto - ry of Je - sus.
Seeking our rest in the mansions of love, Telling the sto - ry of Je - sus.
Casting our crowns at Immanu-el's feet, Telling the sto - ry of Je - sus.

D.S. Bearing with patience, whatever betide, Telling the story of Je - sus.

REFRAIN.

Fearless of danger when He is our guide, Faithful to duty tho' tempted and tried;

Copyright, 1882, by JNO. R. SWENEY.

No. 101. THE HALF HAS NEVER BEEN TOLD.

FRANCIS RIDLEY HAVERGAL. R. E. HUDSON. By per.

1. I know I love Thee better, Lord, Than an - y earthly joy, For
2. I know that Thou art near - er still, Than an - y earthly throng, And
3. Thou hast put gladness in my heart; Then well may I be glad! With -
4. O Sav - iour, precious Saviour mine! What will Thy presence be If

100

THE HALF HAS NEVER BEEN TOLD. Concluded.

Thou hast giv-en me the peace Which noth-ing can de - stroy.
sweet - er is the thought of Thee Than an - y love - ly song.
out the se - cret of Thy love I could not but be sad.
such a life of joy can crown Our walk on earth with Thee?

REFRAIN.

{ The half has never yet been told, Of love so full and free;
{ The half has never yet been told, The blood it cleanseth me.
　　　　　　　　　　　yet been told,　　　　　　cleanseth me.

From "Gems of Gospel Songs."

No. 102.　　HALLOWED SPOT.

Rev. W. Hunter. D. D,

FINE.

1. { There is a spot to me more dear Than native vale or mountain; }
　 { A spot for which affection's tear Springs greateful from its fountain; }

D. C. But where I first my Saviour found And felt my sins forgiv-en.

D. C.

'Tis not where kindred souls abound, Tho' that on earth is Heaven.

2.
Hard was my toil to reach the shore,
　Long toss'd upon the ocean;
Above me was the thunder's roar;
　Beneath the waves' commotion:
Darkly the pall of night was thrown
　Around me, faint with terror;
In that dark hour—how did my groan
　Ascend for years of error!

3.
Sinking and panting as for breath,
　I knew not help was near me; [death,
And cried, "O! save me, Lord, from
　Immortal Jesus, hear me."

Then quick as thought I felt Him mine,
　My Saviour stood before me;
I saw His brightness round me shine,
　And shouted "Glory! Glory!"

4.
O, sacred hour! O, hallow'd spot!
　Where love divine first found me;
Wherever falls my distant lot,
　My heart shall linger round Thee;
And when from earth I rise, to soar
　Up to my home in heaven,
Down will I cast my eyes once more,
　Where I was first forgiven.

101

No. 103. SAVED, SAVED!

Dr. S. G. Wallace.

W. J. Kirkpatrick. By per.

1. Saved from sin, and saved from doubting, Praise the Lord! my soul is free,
2. Wea - ry, long my anxious spir- it, Groped its way in gloomy night,
3. Now is Christ my great-est treasure, Joy-ful - ly His cross I'll bear.
4. Kept by His sus - tain-ing pow-er, High a- bove the billow's foam;

That blest stream of Calvary's fountain, Seen by faith, now cov-ers me.
Knowing not my Sav-iour's mer - it; But at last I've found the light.
No a-mount of earth - ly pleas-ure, Can with this de - light compare.
This new song shall ev - 'ry hour, Cheer me on my jour-ney home.

REFRAIN.

Saved, saved, complete - ly saved, I have the wit-ness with - in;

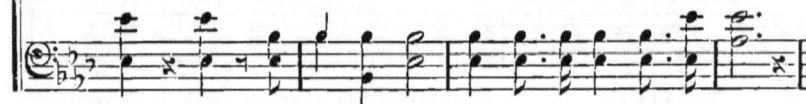

Mo-ment by mo-ment the blood ap- plied, Cleanses my heart from sin.

No. 104. THE ARK FLOATETH BY.

JNO. R. SWENEY. By per.

1. Be-hold the ark of God, Be-hold the o-pen door, O, haste to
2. There safe shalt thou a-bide; There sweet shall be thy rest; And ev'ry
3. And when the waves of wrath A-gain the earth shall fill, Thine ark shall

REFRAIN.

gain that blest a-bode, And rove my soul no more. O come, come to-
wish be sat-is-fied, With full sal-va-tion blest.
ride the sea of fire, And rest on Zi-on's hill.

day, do not lon-ger de-lay, The ark, precious bark, floateth by; The

waves as they roll, Shall not cover thy soul, For Je-sus, thy Saviour, is nigh.

From "Gems of Praise."

105. Tune—"Gates Ajar" 91 Beulah Songs.

1. Beneath the glorious throne above
   The crystal fountain springing,
   A river full of life and love
   Is joy and gladness bringing.

O fount of cleansing flowing free,
That fount is open'd wide to me;
To me, to me, is open'd wide to me,

2. Through all my soul its waters flow,
   Through all my senses stealing;
   And deep within my heart I know
   The consciousness of healing.

3. The barren wastes are fruitful lands,
   The desert blooms with roses;
   And He, the glory of all lands,
   His lovely face discloses.

4. My sun no more goes down by day,
   My moon no more is waning;
   My feet run swift the shining way,
   The heavenly portals gaining.

5. O depth of mercy, breadth of grace,
   O love of God unbounded,
   My soul is lost in sweet amaze,
   O wondrous love confounded.

103

LAND OF PLEASURE.

As sung by Mrs. Inskip.

1. There is a land of pleasure,
   Where streams of joy forever roll,
   'Tis there I have my treasure.
   And there I long to rest my soul.
   Long darkness dwelt around me,
   With scarcely once a cheering ray;
   But since my Saviour found me,
   A light has shone along my way.

2. The vale of tears surrounds me,
   And Jordan's current rolls before;
   Oh how I stand and tremble
   To hear the dismal waters roar!
   Whose hand shall then support me,
   And keep my soul from sinking there?
   From sinking down to darkness,
   And to the regions of despair?

3. The stream shall not affright me,
   Although 'tis deeper than the grave;
   If Jesus will be with me,
   I'll calmly ride on Jordan's wave;
   His word has calmed the ocean,
   His lamp has cheered the gloomy vale,
   Oh may this Friend be with me
   While through the gates of death I sail!

4. Soon the archangel's trumpet
   Shall shake the globe from pole to pole
   And all the wheels of nature
   Shall in a moment cease to roll;
   Then I shall see my Saviour,
   With shining ranks of angels come
   To execute His vengeance,
   And take His faithful servants home.

No. 107.   HE IS CALLING.

Faber.   Arr. by S. J. Vail.

1. There's a wideness in God's mercy, Like the wideness of the sea:
   There's a kindness in His justice Which is more than li-ber-ty

REFRAIN.

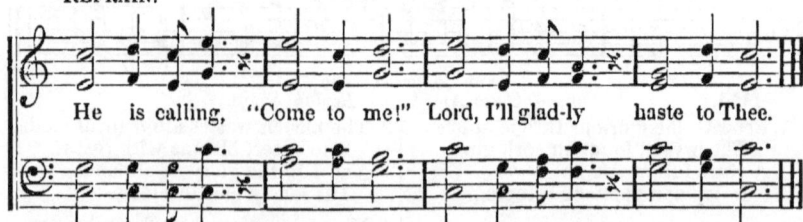

He is calling, "Come to me!" Lord, I'll glad-ly haste to Thee.

2. There is welcome for the sinner,
   And more graces for the good;
   There is mercy with the Saviour;
   There is healing in His blood.

3. For the love of God is broader
   Than the measure of man's mind;

   And the heart of the Eternal,
   Is most wonderful and kind.

4. If our love were but more simple,
   We should take Him at His word;
   And our lives would be all sunshine,
   In the sweetness of our Lord.

No. 108. YONDER, SEE THE LORD DESCENDING.

FINE. | D.C.

1. Yonder! see the Lord descending,
   Hark! His chariot's drawing near;
   Starry worlds before Him rending,
   Flaming troops do now appear.
   Heaven shaking, earth is quaking,
   Mountains fly before His face,
   The dead their dusty beds forsaking,
   Nature sinking in a blaze.

2. Now behold each shining conqueror,
   Rising from their dusty beds,
   Fly to meet their blessed Saviour,
   Glittering crowns upon their heads;

Hear them tell their pleasing story
To their smiling, lovely King,
Glory, glory, glory, glory,
Glory is the song they sing.

3. Once an infant in a manger,
   There the Lord of glory lay;
   No place to lay that little stranger
   But upon the oxen's hay;
   Now He's crowned with a rainbow
   Brighter than a sardine stone:[Him
   He Comes, He comes, the christian sees
   Seated on His great white throne.

No. 109. THE PILGRIM.

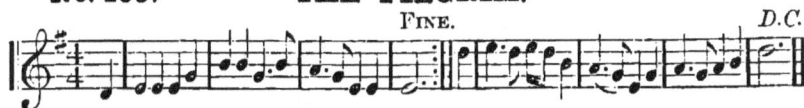

FINE. | D.C.

1. Come all ye wandering pilgrims dear,
   Who are bound for Canaan's land;
   Take courage and fight valiantly,
   Stand forth with sword in hand.
   Our Captain's gone before us,
   The Father's only Son;
   Then pilgrims dear, pray do not fear.
   But let us follow on.

2. We've a dark and howling wilderness,
   'Twixt this and Canaan's shore,
   A land of droughts, and pits, and snares,
   Where hideous dangers roar.
   But Jesus will attend us,
   And guard us in the way
   If enemies examine us,
   He'll teach us what to say.

3. "Good morning, brother traveller,
   Pray tell me what's your name;
   And where is it you're going to,
   Also from whence you came?"

"My name it is Bold Pilgrim,
To Canaan I am bound;
I'm from the howling wilderness,
From that enchanted ground.

4. 'Tis glorious hope upon my head.
   And on my breast a shield;
   With this bright sword I mean to fight
   Until I win the field;
   My feet are shod with gospel peace,
   On which I boldly stand,
   And I'm resolved to fight till death,
   And win fair Canaan's land."

5. "'Tis true, indeed, I am not freed
   From enemies as yet;
   But by the grace of God I stand,
   With them beneath my feet;
   Now I rejoice with a loud voice
   In hope of victory;
   And to God's grace I'll give the praise
   To all eternity."

110. Tune and Chorus,—"In the Sweet By and By."

1. We speak of the land of the blest,
   A country so bright and so fair,
   And oft are its glories confessed,
   But what must it be to be there?

2. We speak of its pathways of gold.
   Its walls decked with jewels so rare,
   Its wonders and pleasures untold,
   But what must it be to be there?

3. We speak of its peace and its love,
   The robes which the glorified wear,
   The songs of the blessed above,
   But what must it be to be there?

4. We speak of its freedom from sin,
   From sorrow, temptation and care,
   From trials without and within,
   But what must it be to be there?

LENOX. H. M.

111.

1. Arise, my soul, arise;
Shake off thy guilty fears;
The bleeding sacrifice
In my behalf appears,
Before the throne my surety stands,
My name is written on his hands,

2. He ever lives above,
For me to intercede;
His all redeeming love,
His precious blood to plead;
His blood atoned for all our race,
And sprinkles now the throne of grace.

3. Five bleeding wounds he bears,
Received on Calvary;
They pour effectual prayers,
They strongly plead for me:
"Forgive him, O forgive," they cry;
"Nor let that ransomed sinner die."

4. The Father hears Him pray,
His dear anointed One;
He cannot turn away
The presence of His Son:
His spirit answers to the blood,
And tells me I am born of God.

5. My God is reconciled;
His pardoning voice I hear;
He owns me for His child.
I can no longer fear:
With confidence I now draw nigh,
And, "Father, Abba, Father," cry.

112.

1. Blow ye the trumpet, blow,
The gladly solemn sound!
Let all the nations know,
To earth's remotest bound,
The year of jubilee is come!
Return, ye ransomed sinners, home.

2. Jesus our great High Priest,
Hath full atonement made:
Ye weary spirits, rest.
Ye mournful souls, be glad;
The year of jubilee is come!
Return, ye ransomed sinners, home.

3. Extol the Lamb of God.
The all-atoning Lamb;
Redemption in His blood
Throughout the world proclaim:
The year of jubilee is come!
Return, ye ransomed sinners, home.

113. Tune and Chorus,—"I am so glad that Jesus loves me."

1.
Jesus loves me, and I know I love Him,
Love brought Him down my poor soul to [redeem;
Yes it was love made Him die on the tree,
O I am certain that Jesus loves me.

2.
If one should ask of me, how could I tell?
Glory to Jesus, I know very well;

God's Holy Spirit with mine doth agree,
Constantly witnessing Jesus loves me.

3.
In this assurance I find sweetest rest,
Trusting in Jesus. I know I am bless'd;
Satan dismayed, from my soul now doth [flee,
When I just tell him that Jesus loves me.

106 J. NICHOLSON.

WRESTLING JACOB.

Rev. Chas. Wesley.   Arr. by Rev. W. McDonald. By per.

1. { Come, O Thou traveller unknown, Whom still I hold, but can-not see; }
   { My compa-ny be-fore is gone, And I am left a-lone with Thee; }

With Thee all night I mean to stay, And wrestle till the break of day.

2. I need not tell Thee who I am;
   My sin and misery declare;
Thyself hast called me by my name;
   Look on Thy hands, and read it there;
But who, I ask Thee, who art Thou?
Tell me Thy name, and tell me now.

3. In vain Thou strugglest to get free,
   I never will unloose my hold;
Art Thou the Man that died for me?
   The secret of Thy love unfold:
Wrestling, I will not let Thee go,
Till I Thy name, Thy nature know

4. Wilt Thou not yet to me reveal
   Thy new, unutterable name?
Tell me, I still beseech Thee, tell;
   To know it now resolved I am:
Wrestling, I will not let Thee go,
Till I Thy name, Thy nature know.

What tho' my shrinking flesh complain,
   And murmur to contend so long?
I rise superior to my pain:
   When I am weak, then I am strong;
And when my all of strength shall fail,
I shall with the God-man prevail.

115.
1. Yield to me now, for I am weak,
   But confident in self-despair;
Speak to my heart, in blessing, speak;
   Be conquer'd by my instant prayer;
Speak, or Thou never hence shall move,
And tell me if Thy name be Love.

2. 'Tis love! 'tis Love! Thou diedst for
   I hear Thy whisper in my heart; [me;
The morning breaks, the shadows flee;
   Pure, universal Love Thou art:
'To me, to all, Thy bowels move,—
Thy nature and Thy name is Love.

3. My prayer has pow'r with God; the
   Unspeakable I now receive; [grace
Through faith I see Thee face to face;
   I see Thee face to face, and live!
In vain I have not wept and strove;
Thy nature and Thy name is Love.

4. I know Thee, Saviour, who Thou art,
   Jesus, the feeble sinner's friend;
Nor wilt Thou with the night depart,
   But stay and love me to the end:
Thy mercies never shall remove;
Thy nature and Thy name is Love.

116.
1. My hope is built on nothing less
Than Jesus' blood and righteousness.
I dare not trust the sweetest frame,
But wholly lean on Jesus' name.

On Christ the solid Rock I stand;
All other ground is sinking sand.

2. When darkness seems to vail his face,
I rest on His unchanging grace;
In every high and stormy gale
My anchor holds within the veil.

3. His oath, His covenant, and blood,
Support me in the 'whelming flood:
When all around my soul gives way,
He then is all my hope and stay.

CLEANSING FOUNTAIN.

COWPER.
WESTERN MELODY.

1. There is a foun-tain fill'd with blood, Drawn from Immanuel's veins,

And sin-ners plung'd beneath that flood Lose all their guil-ty stains.

FINE.

D.S. And sin-ners plung'd beneath that flood Lose all their guil-ty stains.

D.S.

Lose all their guil-ty stains, Lose all their guil-ty stains.

2. The dying thief rejoiced to see
That fountain in his day;
And there may I, though vile as he,
Wash all my sins away.

3. Thou dying Lamb, Thy precious blood
Shall never lose its power,
Till all the ransom'd Church of God
Are saved, to sin no more.

4. E'er since by faith I saw the stream,
Thy flowing wounds supply,
Redeeming love has been my theme,
And shall be till I die.

5. Then in a nobler, sweeter song,
I'll sing Thy power to save,
When this poor lisping, stam'ring tongue
Lies silent in the grave.

118.   Tune.—No. 34 "Beulah Songs."

1. God loved the world of sinners lost
And ruined by the fall!
Salvation full, at highest cost,
He offers free to all.
O 'twas love, 'twas wondrous love!
The love of God to me;
It brought my Saviour from above,
To die on Calvary.

2. E'en now by faith I claim Him mine,
The risen Son of God;
Redemption by His death I find,
And cleansing through the blood.

3. Love brings the glorious fulness in,
And to His saints makes known
The blessed rest from inbred sin,
Through faith in Christ alone.

119.   "I Love to tell the story, 'Twill be my theme in glory."

1. I love to tell the story,
Of unseen things above,
Of Jesus and His glory,
Of Jesus and His love!
I love to tell the Story!
Because I know 'tis true;
It satisfies my longings,
As nothing else would do.

2. I love to tell the story!
More wonderful it seems,
Than all the golden fancies
Of all our golden dreams.
I love to tell the story!
It did so much for me!
And that is just the reason
I tell it now to thee.

NETTLETON.

FINE.   D.C.

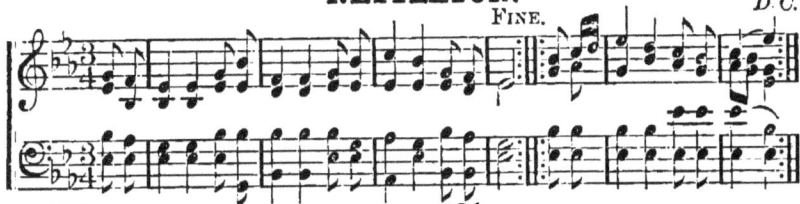

120.

1. Come Thou Fount of every blessing,
   Tune my heart to sing Thy grace;
   Streams of mercy never ceasing,
   Calls for songs of loudest praise.
   Teach me some melodious sonnet,
   Sung by flaming tongues above;
   Praise the mount—I'm fixed upon it—
   Mount of Thy redeeming love.

2. Here I'll raise mine Ebenezer;
   Hither by Thy help I'm come;
   And I hope by Thy good pleasure,
   Safely to arrive at home.
   Jesus sought me when a stranger,
   Wandering from the fold of God,
   He, to rescue me from danger,
   Interposed His precious blood.

3. Oh, to grace how great a debtor,
   Daily I'm constrained to be!
   Let Thy goodness like a fetter,
   Bind my wandering heart to Thee;
   Prone to wander, Lord, I feel it,
   Prone to leave the God I love!
   Here's my heart, O take and seal it;
   Seal it for Thy courts above.

121.

1. Come, ye sinners, poor and needy,
   Weak and wounded, sick and sore;
   Jesus ready stands to save you,
   Full of pity, love and power;
   He is able, He is able,
   He is willing; doubt no more.

2. Now, ye needy, come and welcome;
   God's free bounty glorify;
   True belief and true repentance—
   Every grace that brings you nigh,
   Without money,
   Come to Jesus Christ and buy,

3. Let not conscience make you linger,
   Nor of fitness fondly dream;
   All the fitness He requireth
   Is to feel your need of Him;
   This He gives you—
   'Tis the Spirit's glimmering beam.

4. Come, ye weary, heavy-laden,
   Bruised and mangled by the fall,
   If you tarry till you're better,
   You will never come at all;
   Not the righteous—
   Sinners Jesus came to call.

122.   Tune,—No. 121 "Beulah Songs."

1. What a friend we have in Jesus,
   All our sins and griefs to bear;
   What a privilege to carry
   Everything to God in prayer.
   Oh, what peace we often forfeit,
   Oh, what needless pain we bear—
   All because we do not carry
   Everything to God in prayer.

2. Have we trials and temptations?
   Is there trouble anywhere?
   We should never be discouraged,
   Take it to the Lord in prayer.

Can we find a friend so faithful,
   Who will all our sorrows share?
   Jesus knows our every weakness,
   Take it to the Lord in prayer.

3. Are we weak and heavy laden,
   Cumbered with a load of care?
   Precious Saviour, still our refuge,—
   Take it to the Lord in prayer.
   Do thy friends despise, forsake thee?
   Take it to the Lord in prayer;
   In His arms He'll take and shield thee,
   Thou wilt find a solace there.

123.   Tune,—Page 22 "Winnowed Hymns."

1. My life flows on in endless song,
   Above earth's lamentation,
   I catch the sweet, though far-off hymn,
   That hails a new creation;
   Through all the tumult and the strife,
   I hear the music ringing,
   It finds an echo in my soul—
   How can I keep from singing.

2. What though my joys and comfort die?
   The Lord, my Saviour, liveth;
   What though the darkness gather
   Songs in the night he giveth. [round?

No storms can shake my inmost calm,
   While to that refuge clinging;
   Since Christ is Lord of heaven and earth,
   How can I keep from singing?

3. I lift my eyes; the cloud grows thin;
   I see the blue above it;
   And day by day this pathway smooths,
   Since first I learned to love it.
   The peace of Christ makes fresh my [heart,
   A fountain ever springing;
   All things are mine since I am His—
   How can I keep from singing?

109

SESSIONS. L. M.

L. O. EMERSON.

124.

1. Lord, I am Thine, entirely Thine,
Purchased and saved by blood divine:
With full consent Thine I would be,
And own Thy sovereign right in me.

2. Grant one poor sinner more a place
Among the children of Thy grace;
A wretched sinner, lost to God,
But ransomed by Immanuel's blood.

3. Thine would I live, Thine would I die,
Be Thine through all eternity;
The vow is past beyond repeal.
And now I set the solemn seal.
[blood
4. Here, at that cross where flows the
That bought my guilty soul for God,
Thee, my new Master, now I call,
And consecrate to thee my all,

125.

1. I thirst, Thou wounded Lamb of God,
To wash me in Thy cleansing blood;
To dwell within Thy wounds; then pain
Is sweet, and life or death is gain.

2. Take my poor heart, and let it be
Forever closed to all but Thee:
Seal Thou my breast, and let me wear
That pledge of love forever there.

3. How blest are they who still abide
Close sheltered in Thy bleeding side!
[rive,
Who thence their life and strength de-
And by Thee move, and in Thee live.
[flow,
4. Hence our hearts melt, our eyes o'er-
Our words are lost, nor will we know

Nor will we think of aught beside;
"My Lord, my Love is crucified."

126.

1. While life prolongs its precious light,
Mercy is found, and peace is given;
But soon, ah, soon approaching night
Shall blot out every hope of heaven.

2. While God invites, how blest the day!
[sound!
How sweet the gospel's charming
Come sinners, haste, O haste away,
While yet a pardoning God is found.

3. Soon, borne on time's most rapid wing,
Shall death command you to the
Before His bar your spirits bring, [grave,
And none be found to hear or save.

4. In that lone land of deep despair,
No Sabbath's heavenly light shall rise,
No God regard your bitter prayer,
No Saviour call you to the skies.

127.

1. Of Him who did salvation bring,
I could forever think and sing;
Arise, ye needy,—He'll relieve;
Arise, ye guilty,—He'll forgive.

2. Ask but His grace, and lo, 'tis given;
Ask, and He turns your hell to heaven:
Though sin and sorrow wound my soul,
Jesus, Thy balm will make it whole,

3. To shame our sins He blushed in blood;
He closed His eyes to show us God:
Let all the world fall down and know
That none but God such love can show.

FOREST. L. M.

A. Chapin.

128.

1. Show pity, Lord, O Lord, forgive;
Let a repenting rebel live:
Are not Thy mercies large and free?
May not a sinner trust in Thee?

2. My crimes are great, but don't surpass,
The power and glory of Thy grace;
Great God, Thy nature hath no bound,
So let Thy pardoning love be found.

3. O wash my soul from every sin,
And make my guilty conscience clean;
Here on my heart the burden lies,
And past offenses pain my eyes.

4. Yet save a trembling sinner, Lord,
[word,
Whose hope, still hovering round Thy
Would light on some sweet promise there
Some sure support against despair.

129.

1. I know that my Redeemer lives;
What joy the blest assurance gives!
He lives, He lives, who once was dead;
He lives, my everlasting Head!

2. He lives, to bless me with His love;
He lives, to plead for me above;
He lives, my hungry soul to feed;
He lives, to help in time of need.

3. He lives and grants me daily breath;
He lives, and I shall conquer death;
He lives, my mansion to prepare;
He lives, to bring me safely there.

4. He lives, all glory to His name;
He lives, my Saviour, still the same;
What joy the blest assurance gives,
I know that my Redeemer lives!

130.

1. He leadeth me! oh, blessed thought,
Oh, words with heavenly comfort
Whate'er I do, where'er I be, [fraught!
Still 'tis God's hand that leadeth me.

He leadeth me! He leadeth me!
By His own hand He leadeth me!
His faithful foll'wer I would be;
For by His hand He leadeth me.

2. Lord, I would clasp Thy hand in mine,
Nor ever murmur or repine—
Content, whatever lot I see.
Since 'tis my God that leadeth me;

3. And when my task on earth is done,
When, by Thy grace the victory's won,
E'en death's cold wave I will not flee,
Since God thro' Jordan leadeth me.

131. Tune,—Page 36 "Garner."

1. Shall we meet beyond the river,
Where the surges cease to roll?
Where in all the bright forever,
Sorrow ne'er shall press the soul.

Shall we meet, shall we meet,
Shall we meet beyond the river?
Shall we meet beyond the river,
Where the surges cease to roll.

2. Shall we meet in that blest harbor,
When our stormy voyage is o'er?
Shall we meet and cast the anchor,
By the bright celestial shore.

3. Shall we meet in yonder city,
Where the towers of crystal shine?
Where the walls are all of jasper,
Built by workmanship divine?

4. Shall we meet there many a loved one,
That was torn from our embrace?
Shall we listen to their voices,
And behold them face to face?

5. Shall we meet with Christ our Saviour,
When He comes to claim His own?
Shall we know His blessed favor,
And sit down upon His throne?

111

WARE. L. M.

George Kingsley.

132.

1. O that my load of sin were gone!
O that I could at last submit
At Jesus' feet to lay it down—
To lay my soul at Jesus' feet!

2. Rest for my soul I long to find:
Saviour of all, if mine Thou art,
Give me Thy meek and lowly mind,
And stamp Thine image on my heart.

3. Break off the yoke of inbred sin,
And fully set my spirit free;
I cannot rest till pure within,
Till I am wholly lost in Thee.

4. Fain would I learn of Thee, my God,
Thy light and easy burden prove,
The cross all stained with hallowed
The labor of Thy dying love. [blood,

5. I would, but Thou must give the power,
My heart from every sin release;
Bring near, bring near the joyful hour,
And fill me with Thy perfect peace,

133.

1. From every stormy wind that blows,
From every swelling tide of woes,
There is a calm, a sure retreat;
'Tis found beneath the mercy-seat.

2. There is a place where Jesus sheds
The oil of gladness on our heads.

A place than all besides more sweet:
It is the blood-bought mercy-seat.

3. There is a scene where spirits blend,
Where friend holds fellowship with
[friend:
Though sundered far, by faith they meet
Around one common mercy-seat.

4. There, there on eagle wings we soar,
And sin and sense molest no more;[greet,
And heaven comes down our souls to
While glory crowns the mercy-seat.

134.

1. When I survey the wondrous cross,
On which the Prince of glory died,
My richest gain I count but loss,
And pour contempt on all my pride.

2. Forbid it, Lord, that I should boast,
Save in the death of Christ, my God;
All the vain things that charm me most,
I sacrifice them to His blood.

3. See, from His head, His hands, His feet,
Sorrow and love flow mingled down:
Did e'er such love and sorrow meet,
Or thorns compose so rich a crown?

4. Were the whole realm of nature mine,
That were a present far too small;
Love so amazing, so divine,
Demands my soul, my life, my all.

135.   Tune,—No. 138 "Ark of Praise."

1. O happy day that fixed my choice
On Thee, my Saviour and my God!
Well may this glowing heart rejoice,
And tell its raptures all abroad.

Happy day, when Jesus washed my sins away:
He taught me how to watch and pray,
And live rejoicing every day;
Happy day, when Jesus washed my sins away.

2. 'Tis done, the great transaction's done;
I am my Lord's, and He is mine;

He drew me, and I followed on,
Charm'd to confess the voice Divine.

3. Now rest, my long-divided heart;
Fixed on this blissful center, rest;
Nor ever from thy Lord depart;
With Him of every good possess'd.
[vow,

4. High heaven, that heard the solemn
That vow renewed shall daily hear,
Till in life's latest hour I bow,
And bless in death a bond so dear.

112

AZMON. C.M.

136.

1. O for a heart to praise my God,
A heart from sin set free!
A heart that always feels Thy blood,
So freely spilt for me.

2. A heart resigned, submissive, meek,
My great Redeemer's throne;
Where only Christ is heard to speak,
Where Jesus reigns alone.

3. O for a lowly, contrite heart.
Believing, true, and clean.
Which neither life nor death can part
From Him that dwells within.

4. A heart in every thought renewed,
And full of love divine.
Perfect, and right, and pure, and good,
A copy, Lord, of Thine.

137.

1. All hail the power of Jesus' name!
Let angels prostrate fall;
Bring forth the royal diadem,
And crown Him Lord of all.

2. Ye chosen seed of Israel's race,
Ye ransomed from the fall,
Hail Him who saves you by His grace,
And crown Him Lord of all.

3. Let every kindred, every tribe,
On this terrestrial ball,
To Him all majesty ascribe,
And crown Him Lord of all.

4. O that with yonder sacred throng
We at His feet may fall!
We'll join the everlasting song,
And crown Him Lord of all.

140.

1. Jesus, Lover of my soul,
Let me to Thy bosom fly,
While the nearer waters roll,
While the tempest still is high!
Hide me, O my Saviour, hide,
Till the storm of life is past;
Safe into the haven guide,
O receive my soul at last.

2. Other refuge have I none;
Hangs my helpless soul on Thee:
Leave, O leave me not alone,
Still support and comfort me:

138.

1. Jesus, Thine all-victorious love
Shed in my heart abroad:
Then shall my feet no longer rove,
Rooted and fixed in God.

2. O that in me the sacred fire
Might now begin to glow,
Burn up the dross of base desire
And make the mountains flow!

3. O that it now from heaven might fall,
And all my sins consume!
Come, Holy Ghost, for Thee I call;
Spirit of burning come!

4. Refining fire, go through my heart;
Illuminate my soul;
Scatter Thy life through every part,
And sanctify the whole.

139.

1. O for a thousand tongues, to sing
My great Redeemer's praise;
The glories of my God and King,
The triumphs of His grace!

2. My gracious Master and my God,
Assist me to proclaim,
To Spread through all the earth abroad,
The honors of Thy name.

3. Jesus! the name that charms our fears,
That bids our sorrows cease,
'Tis music in the sinner's ears,
'Tis life, and health, and peace.

4. He breaks the power of canceled sin,
He sets the prisoner free;
His blood can make the foulest clean,
His blood availed for me.

"Tune,—Martyn."

All my trust on Thee is stayed,
All my help from Thee I bring;
Cover my defenceless head
With the shadow of Thy wing!

3. Thou, O Christ, art all I want:
More than all in Thee I find;
Raise the fallen, cheer the faint,
Heal the sick, and lead the blind.

Just and holy is Thy name,
I am all unrighteousness:
False and full of sin I am,
Thou art full of truth and grace.

CROSS AND CROWN. C. M.

G. W. Allen.   A. Chapin.

141.

1. Must Jesus bear the cross alone,
   And all the world go free?
   No, there's a cross for every one,
   And there's a cross for me.

2. How happy are the saints above,
   Who once went sorrowing here!
   But now they taste unmingled love,
   And joy without a tear.

3. The consecrated cross I'll bear,
   Till death shall set me free:
   And then go home my crown to wear,
   For there's a crown for me.

142.

1. Come, humble sinner, in whose breast
   A thousand thoughts revolve, [ed,
   Come, with your guilt and fear oppress-
   And make this last resolve:—

2. I'll go to Jesus, though my sin
   Like mountains round me close;
   I know His courts, I'll enter in,
   Whatever may oppose.

3. Prostrate I'll lie before His throne,
   And there my guilt confess;
   I'll tell Him, I'm a wretch undone
   Without His sovereign grace.

143.

1. Am I a soldier of the cross,
   A follower of the Lamb,
   And shall I fear to own His cause,
   Or blush to speak His name?

2. Must I be carried to the skies,
   On flowery beds of ease,
   While others fought to win the prize,
   And sailed through bloody seas?

3. Are there no foes for me to face?
   Must I not stem the flood?
   Is this vile world a friend to grace,
   To help me on to God?

4. Sure I must fight, if I would reign:
   Increase my courage, Lord;
   I'll bear the toil, endure the pain,
   Supported by Thy word.

144.   Tune,—Page 28 "Winnowed Hymns."

1. To the cross of Christ, my Saviour.
   I had brought my weary soul,
   Burdened, faint and broken-hearted.
   Praying, "Jesus make me whole."

   Glory, glory be to Jesus,
   I am counting all but dross;
   I have found a full salvation,
   I am resting at the cross.

2. At the cross, while prostrate lying,
   Jesus' blood flowed o'er my soul,
   All my guilt and sin were covered
   And He whispered, Child be whole.

3. At the cross I'm calmly trusting,
   Every moment now is sweet;
   I am tasting of His glory,
   I am resting at His feet.

145.   Tune.—"Hendon."

1. Children of the heavenly King,
   As we journey let us sing.
   Sing our Saviour's worthy praise,
   Glorious in His works and ways.

2. We are traveling home to God,
   In the way our fathers trod;
   They are happy now, and we
   Soon their happiness shall see.

3. Fear not, brethren, joyful stand
   On the borders of our land;
   Jesus Christ, our Father's Son,
   Bids us undismayed go on.

4. Lord, obediently we'll go,
   Gladly leaving all below;
   Only Thou our Leader be,
   And we still will follow Thee.

114

AVON. C. M.

Hugh Wilson.

146.

1. Forever here my rest shall be,
Close to Thy bleeding side;
This all my hope, and all my plea
"For me the Saviour died."

2. My dying Saviour, and my God,
Fountain for guilt and sin.
Sprinkle me ever with Thy blood,
And cleanse and keep me clean.

3. Wash me, and make me thus Thine
Wash me, and mine Thou art; [own;
Wash me, but not my feet alone,
My hands, my head, my heart.

4. The atonement of Thy blood apply,
Till faith to sight improve;
Till hope in full fruition die,
And all my soul be love.

147.

1. Alas! and did my Saviour bleed?
And did my Sovereign die?
Tould He devote that sacred head
For such a worm as I?

2. Was it for crimes that I have done,
He groaned upon the tree?
Amazing pity! grace unknown!
And love beyond degree!

3. Well might the sun in darkness hide,
And shut His glories in,
When Christ, the mighty Maker,died,
For man, the creature's sin.

4. Thus might I hide my blushing face,
While His dear cross appears;
Dissolve my heart in thankfulness,
And melt mine eyes to tears.

148.

1. O for a closer walk with God,
A calm and heavenly frame;
A light to shine upon the road
That leads me to the Lamb!

2. Where is the blessedness I knew,
When first I saw the Lord?

Where is the soul-refreshing view
Of Jesus and His word?

3. Return, O holy Dove, return,
Sweet messenger of rest!
I hate the sins that made Thee mourn,
And drove Thee from my breast.

4. The dearest idol I have known,
Whate'er that idol be,
Help me to tear it from Thy throne,
And worship only Thee.

149.

1. Come, Holy Spirit, heavenly Dove,
With all Thy quickening powers;
Kindle a flame of sacred love
In these cold hearts of ours.

2. Look how we grovel here below,
Fond of these earthly toys;
Our souls, how heavily they go,
To reach eternal joys.

3. Father, and shall we ever live
At this poor dying rate,
Our love so faint, so cold to Thee,
And Thine to us so great?

4. Come, Holy Spirit, heavenly Dove,
With all Thy quickening powers;
Come, shed abroad a Saviour's love,
And that shall kindle ours.

150.

1. O for a faith that will not shrink,
Though pressed by every foe,
That will not tremble on the brink
Of any earthly woe!

2. A faith that shines more bright and
When tempests rage without; [clear
That when in danger knows no fear,
In darkness feels no doubt;

3. Lord, give us such a faith as this,
And then, whate'er may come,
We'll taste, e'en here, the hallowed bliss
Of an eternal home.

BOYLSTON. S. M.

Moderato.

L. Mason.

151.

1. And can I yet delay,
   My little all to give?
   To tear my soul from earth away
   For Jesus to receive?

2. Nay, but I yield, I yield;
   I can hold out no more;
   I sink, by dying love compelled,
   And own Thee conqueror.

3. Though late, I all forsake;
   My friends, my all, resign;
   Gracious Redeemer, take, O take,
   And seal me ever Thine.

4. Come, and possess me whole,
   Nor hence again remove;
   Settle and fix my wavering soul
   With all Thy weight of love.

152.

1. A charge to keep I have,
   A God to glorify;
   A never-dying soul to save,
   And fit it for the sky.

2. To serve the present age,
   My calling to fulfill,—
   O may it all my powers engage,
   To do my Master's will.

3. Arm me with jealous care,
   As in Thy sight to live;
   And O, thy servant, Lord, prepare,
   A strict account to give.

4. Help me to watch and pray,
   And on Thyself rely,
   Assured, if I my trust betray,
   I shall forever die.

153.

1. Grace! 'tis a charming sound,
   Harmonious to the ear;
   Heaven with the echo shall resound,
   And all the earth shall hear.

2. Grace first contrived a way
   To save rebellious man;
   And all the steps that grace display,
   Which drew the wondrous plan.

3. Grace taught my roving feet
   To tread the heavenly road;
   And new supplies each hour I meet,
   While pressing on to God.

4. Grace all the work shall crown
   Through everlasting days;
   It lays in heaven the topmost stone,
   And well deserves our praise.

No. 154.   THE LION OF JUDAH.

English Melody.

1. Twas Jesus my Saviour, who died on the tree, To open a fountain for sinners like me.
2. And when I was willing with all things to part, He gave me my bounty, His love in my heart;
3. And when with the ransomed by Jesus my head, From fountain to fountain I then shall be led.
4. Come, sinners to Jesus no longer de-lay, A full, free salvation he of-fers to day;

His blood is that fountain which pardon bestows, And cleanses the foulest wherever it flows.
So now I am joined with the conquering band, Who are marching to glory at Jesus command.
I'll fall at His feet and His mercy a-dore, And sing of the blood of the cross evermore.
Arouse your dark spirits, awake from your dream, And Christ will support you in coming to Him.

REFRAIN.

For the Li-on of Judah shall break ev'ry chain, And give us the vict'ry a-gain and a-gain.

No. 155. WHEN THE BRIDEGROOM COMES?

1. O, brother will you meet me
   When the Bridegroom comes?
   O, brother will you meet me,
   When He comes, when He comes,
   O, brother will you meet me,
   O, brother will you meet me,

O, brother will you meet me,
When He comes, when He comes?
2. O, sister will you meet me, etc.
3. Won't that be a happy meeting, etc.
4. Are you ready for the Bridegroom,
   When He comes, when He comes, etc.

156.   Tune,—"Toplady."

1. Rock of Ages, cleft for me,
   Let me hide myself in Thee;
   Let the water and the blood,
   From Thy wounded side which flow'd,
   Be of sin the double cure,—
   Save from wrath and make me pure.
2. Could my tears forever flow,
   Could my zeal no languor know
   These for sin could not atone;

Thou must save, and Thou alone·
In my hand no price I bring;
Simply to Thy cross I cling.
3. While I draw this fleeting breath,
   When my eyes shall close in death,
   When I rise to worlds unknown,
   And behold Thee on Thy throne,
   Rock of Ages, cleft for me,
   Let me hide myself in Thee.

157.   Tune,—"Bethany."

1. Nearer, my God, to Thee
   Nearer to Thee;
   E'en though it be a cross,
   That raiseth me,
   Still all my song shall be,
   ‖: Nearer, my God, to Thee, :‖
   Nearer to Thee.
2. Though like the wanderer,
   The sun gone down,
   Darkness be over me,
   My rest a stone;

Yet in my dreams I'd be,
‖: Nearer, my God, to Thee, :‖
Nearer to Thee.

3. There let the way appear,
   Steps unto heaven;
   All that Thou sendest me
   In mercy given;
   Angels to beckon me,
   ‖: Nearer, my God, to Thee, :‖
   Nearer to Thee.

No. 158. I LEFT IT ALL WITH JESUS.

Words and Music Adapted and Arranged.

1. O, I left it all with Jesus long ago, long ago, My sinfulness I brought Him and my woe,
2. O, I leave it all with Jesus for He knows, for He knows, Just how to take the bitter from life's woes,
3. O, I leave it all with Jesus day by day, day by day, My faith can firmly trust Him, Come what may,

And when by faith I saw Him on the tree, And heard His still small whisper,"'Tis for thee,"
And how to gild the tear-drop with His smile, To make the desert garden bloom a - while,
For hope has dropped her anchor, found her rest, Within the calm sure haven of His breast.

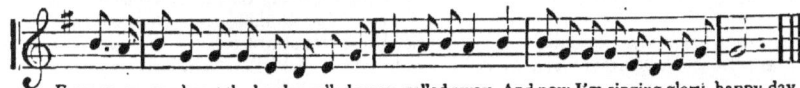

From my weary heart the burden rolled away, rolled away, And now I'm singing glory, happy day.
Then, with all my weakness leaning on His might, on His might, My soul sings hallelujah, all is light.
    And   oh! 'tis joy of heaven to   a - bide, to abide, Close to my dear Redeemer, at His side.

117

WM. H. KEYSER & CO., MUSIC TYPOGRAPHERS, 921 ARCH ST., PHILADA.

INDEX.

Titles in Small Caps,—First lines in Roman,—Refrains in Italic.

www.ingramcontent.com/pod-product-compliance
Lightning Source LLC
Chambersburg PA
CBHW032240080426
42735CB00008B/939